Huts for Houses
A Forres Squatter's Childhood

Huts for Houses
A Forres Squatter's Childhood

by

Violet Fraser

J & J Publishing

Published by J & J Publishing

First Published in Scotland in 2012 by
J & J Publishing
Ty Crwn, East Grange, Kinloss, Forres, Moray, IV36 2UD

First reprint 2012
Second reprint 2012
Third reprint 2013

Bespoke Publishing

Typeset by J & J Publishing
Design by J & J Publishing 01 343 850 123
Picture repair, enhancements & jacket design by Harvey Pettit
harveypettit@gmail.com
Proofread by Susan Kemp
Printed by MPG Printgroup, UK

ISBN: 978-0-9543891-7-8

Acknowledgements

No book is ever the product of one person's efforts and certainly this one was no different. It would never have become reality without the help and suggestions of many supportive friends and family. My biggest thanks go to my husband, Gordon, and my youngest daughter, Joanne, for their continued support and encouragement. I would also like to acknowledge other members of my family, including my oldest daughter Lindsay.

My thanks go to Ross Dalziel for his wartime memories and insight; to Raymond Miller, Veronica Musik Tomlins and Peter Jones for the photos; extracts from Roger Kelly's webpage on Polish Forces in Scotland; Graeme Wilson of the Moray Council's archive service for the *Forres, Elgin & Nairn Gazette* newspaper cuttings and the kind permission for the use of these from the Scottish Provincial Press.

I have wanted to write this book since I was in my twenties. A big thank you to Jacqui Jones, J & J Publishing, for her help and understanding and for getting this book published - at last.

Dedications

To Mam & Dad Fraser

Happiness is fleeting
But sorrow is forever
Love lingers on
When a loved one is gone

Tears fall like rain
A never ending stream
But the well never runs dry
Better by far to dream

by Violet Fraser

Introduction

IN 1940 the Air Ministry requisitioned farmland at, and adjacent to, Balnageith to build RAF Forres where thousands of Aircrew for Bomber Command were trained for the war effort. RAF Forres, known locally as Balnageith, was one of the satellite operational training units for nearby RAF Kinloss.

The grass surfaced airfield continued to operate until October 1944 when it was no longer needed by the RAF. In November 1944, after clearing the station of all stores and equipment, the Air Ministry loaned most of the domestic facilities to the War Department for use as a prisoner of war camp, where it served in this capacity until mid 1947.

Erected in 1997, this cairn commemorates those who served at RAF Forres
1940-1944 and the presence of the Polish Armed Forces 1945-1947
Courtesy of Peter Jones

From 1945 Polish ex-prisoners of war were sent to the camp to live in the huts that had been built around the now redundant airfield. Forced to fight on the German side they had become temporary prisoners of war (POWs) in Eastern Europe and on the Russian front. After capture by the Allies, the men had been shipped to ports on the east coast of Britain.

Italian POWs came to Moray sometime between 1942-1943 when the airfield was in full use by the RAF. They were housed in camps specially built for them in places such as Dallas and Dunphail, where they lived throughout the war. These camps were demolished after the war.

Ross Dalziel, whose family owned a tomato farm called Grovita, which was close to the Balnaferry huts, recalls that many POWs travelled to the north by train and those coming to Forres were marched from the station under armed guard. Ross was a young lad of 10 when he first saw them near his home at Balnaferry. Seeing the unkempt and war-worn hordes shuffling through the town toward their accommodation left an indelible mark on his memory. Ross says:

'The sight of columns of bedraggled men walking, limping and some being helped by their comrades has lived with me for over 60 years.Their uniforms were filthy, torn and some had no uniform but were in civilian clothing. Few had overcoats and some had no proper footwear and had sacking or other material wrapped round their feet to protect them. They were all unshaven and looked really fearsome to a 9-10 year old.

It must have been summer 1945 when one batch of prisoners were being marched under armed guard over the railway bridge up the Grantown road when they spotted a field of carrots at Thornhill. They broke ranks and climbed the fence into the field and started eating the carrots straight out of the ground. The guards fired warning shots over their heads but it took some time to get the hungry prisoners back into the road and on up to their prison camp.

Once in the camp each batch of POWs was given a proper meal (the majority were and looked starving). This was probably the first decent meal they had eaten in a very long time. They were then taken to the personal cleansing centre, a brick building, which smelt like a modern laundry, where they were given shower facilities and they were able to shave and get their hair cut. They were issued with new, warm clothing, boots and clean bedding and marched to their huts still under armed guard.

The huts were situated in the environs of the airfield and they were tucked away close to the woods, which helped camouflage them when they were part of RAF Forres. Each hut was about 60 feet x 20 feet (18m x 6m) and housed between 20 and 30 prisoners.

Our home, Balnaferry House, was situated very close to the Balnaferry camp, as it became called. I remember cycling down to Forres with my sister, Marjorie, to buy cigarettes and bread. We would cycle back up to the camp, go to the gates and swap cigarettes and slices of bread for German, Ukraine, Polish and other Baltic state currency. We used to watch the prisoners of war marching up and down the roads, going back and fore to the mess hall for their meals.

In the winter during the war the RAF boys would be going back and fore to the huts at Sanquhar and Anderson Crescent. On this journey they walked along a path beside the dyke which ran along below the north side of the tomato farm. In the winter they used to jump up and steal from our coal stocks, which we used for steam-sterilising the glasshouse soil. This was to augment their supplies for their billets' stoves. We knew this because the manager used to whitewash the coal next to the dyke and there were gaps in the morning, coal having been taken. My father turned a blind eye to this; it was wartime and everyone needed help.

During and after the war, we sold most of our tomatoes wholesale to a local company, Gordon & MacPhail, but we opened two afternoons a week to allow locals to buy direct from the farm. Queues would form on these days for fresh tomatoes; we sold the early ones for a shilling (5p) a pound.

When the local Forres men came home and found that there was nowhere to live they moved into the huts too. There were also squatters in the buildings of the Navy, Army and Air Force Institute (NAAFI), opposite the main camp gates, where Ferry Road houses are now.

Once the squatters moved in, each camp and group of huts was given a different name by the locals. They were called the Sanquhar huts, Burdshaugh huts (where Violet, the author, lived), Balnaferry huts, Whiterow huts, Thornhill huts and Balnageith huts. (The locations of these are shown on the aerial photograph, page xviii.)

My wife to be, Vallie Forbes, lived above her parent's family business, Deas the Bakers. After the war, displaced Poles regularly got use of the bakehouse on a Saturday and they made wonderful bread for themselves. The loaves were plaited and decorated in ways that Vallie had never seen before. The only fancy loaf she had seen up till then was the usual sheaf of corn shape made for harvest thanksgiving in church.

I recall the Italian prisoners of war making rings out of aluminium and coloured broken glass and they also made brass aeroplanes, which they sold locally, mainly to young people. Vallie longed for one of those rings but never got one.

Once the war was over, many Poles stayed in Forres and some moved into empty camp huts. Many of them worked here and at one time about 20 Poles had businesses in the town. One of them, Mr Radnor, became the official barber at RAF Kinloss and Mr Kaminski started up in business as an electrician.

Most of the huts have now disappeared but there are a few remaining at Balnagieth and one or two remain at Whiterow but they have collapsed and planning permission is being sought for new houses to be built on this site. These and about eight up the little road to Mannachie were about the furthest away from the main camp, the others being where Mannachie Terrace is now (about another eight) and the same in the top corner of the fields where Anderson Crescent is now.'

AFTER the war ended in September 1945, the Italian POWs were repatriated and in 1946 RAF Forres was used as a resettlement camp for those from the Polish Armed Forces who had fought against Germany from the UK. Many did not wish to return to a communist Poland created as a result of the 1945 Yalta Agreement between Stalin, Roosevelt and Churchill.

Commemorative plaque on the Cairn erected in 1997 for those
who served at RAF Forres 1940-1944 and the presence of the
Polish Armed Forces who were billeted on the site between 1945-1947.
Courtesy of Peter Jones

From early on in the war, the bulk of the Polish Army in Great Britain had been resettled in Scotland under real threat of German attacks so the newly-arrived Poles were warmly welcomed as they immediately set to work defending their hosts' land, although this sentiment did not last as it was feared that when the war ended the Poles would take jobs and homes.

In her book, *The Lion and the Eagle,* Dr Diana Henderson says of the Poles in Scotland:

'Scots empathy with the natives of an invaded country and Celtic natural hospitality soon overcame the suspicion of strange uniforms and an equally strange language. The Poles themselves contributed substantially to surmounting these barriers. Their efforts with the language and the Scots accent, largely self-taught, enabled them to begin to communicate with the local communities and it was soon found that the newcomers were not only good looking but had an engaging charm and impeccable manners. Their grooming was immaculate and they even wore aftershave. Scots lassies had seldom seen the like before.'

HOPEFULLY this introduction provides a suitable foil for Violet's story about the 'squatters' who moved into the huts on the then redundant airfield. They formed a significant part of the history of the immediate post World War II period, not only locally but nationally.

COUNTY OF MORAY
NATIONAL REGISTRATION OFFICE
ELGIN

S.A.   151968

NATIONAL REGISTRATION

IDENTITY CARD

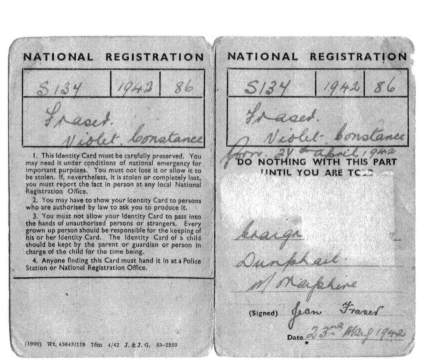

NATIONAL REGISTRATION

S134   1942   86

Fraser.
Violet Constance

1. This Identity Card must be carefully preserved. You may need it under conditions of national emergency for important purposes. You must not lose it or allow it to be stolen. If, nevertheless, it is stolen or completely lost, you must report the fact in person at any local National Registration Office.

2. You may have to show your Identity Card to persons who are authorised by law to ask you to produce it.

3. You must not allow your Identity Card to pass into the hands of unauthorised persons or strangers. Every grown up person should be responsible for the keeping of his or her Identity Card. The Identity Card of a child should be kept by the parent or guardian or person in charge of the child for the time being.

4. Anyone finding this Card must hand it in at a Police Station or National Registration Office.

(1909) Wt. 45645/119 78m 4/42 J. & J. G. S3-2259

NATIONAL REGISTRATION

S134   1942   86

Fraser.
Violet Constance

from 24th April 1942

DO NOTHING WITH THIS PART UNTIL YOU ARE TOLD

Craige
Dunphail.
N Morayshire

(Signed) Jean Fraser

Date 23rd May 1942

Veronica & Ian (Sheppy) Musik & friends
outside the Sanquhar huts early 1950
Courtesy of Veronica Musik Tomlins

One of the derelict huts at Balnageith 2012
Courtesy of Peter Jones

Ian (Sheppy) Musik, Veronica Musik & Peter Charkiewicz
Outside one of the Sanquhar huts in 1951
Courtesy of Veronica Musik Tomlins

Derelict huts at Balnageith 2012
Courtesy of Peter Jones

Aerial photograph of Forres 1967
looking in a South South Westerly direction

Balnageith camp
(derelict huts present 2012)

Whiterow huts
(derelict huts present 2012)

NAAFI
(New Ferry Road)

Thornhill huts

Grantown Rd

High Street

Market Cross

Balnaferry
huts

Sanquhar huts
now Mannachie Terrace

Grovita
Tomato Farm

Burdshaugh huts

Anderson Crescent

Roysvale Place
Violet's home when
she left the huts

Chapter 1
1942

Jean Tough (*Mum*) with me (*Violet*)
1 year 3 months old

My story begins in April 1942, when I was born in Leanchoil, a small cottage hospital on the outskirts of my home town of Forres in north-east Scotland. My parents, Jean Tough and James Fraser only married the year before. There was no time to find a home for us because my father was always away at sea in the Royal Navy. These were the dark days of the war and I was taken home to Granny and Grandad Tough's tiny cottage nine miles outside Forres, up towards Dunphail. This house was called Craigroy Cottage and it is still there today.

Granny Tough with Mum (*Jean*)

Granny Tough had six children, three boys, three girls, my mam Jean being the eldest. The cottage consisted of the family room, which was on the left, just inside the front door. This was the heart of the house. Everything was done in this room. It had a big black range on which granny did all the cooking, baking and constant boiling of water for various tasks, things we take for granted today. At the back of this room was a bedroom for granny and grandad. Beyond the entrance to the family room was another door, which led to a tiny room where my two aunties slept. Between these two doors in the tiny hall there was a ladder, which went straight up to the attic. This is where the three sons of the family slept. So, you may ask, where did mam and I go? We went through a dividing wall, which led into Mrs McSteven's cottage next door. She was a good friend of the family and my mother and I were given a room for the duration of the war in her part of the cottage. This then, was the life I would live with my mother Jean, Granny and Grandad Tough, my Uncles Charlie, John and Wilson and my Aunties Margaret and Bess; although Bess, having joined the Women's Land Army, was soon to live at their camp at Dunphail. My father Jimmy was fighting the war so I didn't see much of him during this time.

My memories of those years have stayed with me all my life and my uncles and aunts are amazed at my recall of them, as I needed them to verify those memories.

I had a wonderful childhood there and I think I was totally spoilt by my family, being the first grandchild in both the Fraser and Tough families. But now I realise how hard a life Granny Tough had.

Granny Tough's cottage was situated end on to the road that ran downhill to Forres and uphill to the school and McGillivray's Farm, Burntack and eventually to the Loch of the Romach from which the water for Forres was supplied. She had a front and back garden. On one side she grew flowers taller than I was and I grow them in my own garden today. The other side was planted with rasps *(raspberries)*, blackcurrants and some vegetables and we also had a damson tree. Although it is an old-fashioned fruit now, I still look for it in old gardens. Three steps and we were into the woods where my grandad had made quite a big clearing and planted more vegetables because of the shortages of foodstuffs during the war. He also had his main sheds there for firewood, saw benches and saws. We had a chicken run there too and, believe it or not, that was where we had our outhouse *(toilet)*.

The back of the cottage was just rough grass. This was where the washing was done. There was no water in the house but we had a standpipe at the side of the cottage, cold water obviously. There was a ring of good-sized stones on a bare bit of ground and this was where granny did her washing. A fire was lit in the stones and a big black witchy style pot was put on to boil. It must have taken all day to do the wash. The small stuff was hung on clothes lines and the sheets were spread over the grass to bleach and dry in the sun. In the winter they would just be hung on the lines and take their chances.

I must tell you that my Auntie Margaret is only seven years older than me so was just a little girl when I was a young child myself. She tells me that she had her own little ring of stones in a little shed to the side of the drying green. She used to light her own wee fire and boil tiny potatoes on it. When I asked her what she did with them afterwards, she said, "Well I ate them of course!" Stupid question … .

Auntie Margaret in the 1940s

I don't have memories of my two older uncles, Charlie and John, in those years because they were off to work before I surfaced in the mornings and I was in bed before they came home. They must have had a long day because they had to cycle down to the Altyre estate, where they worked at Riddochs sawmill.

I must tell you a little about my Great Grandad Tough. In his early years he went to Canada to preach the Gospel, as he was a lay preacher but came back home to marry. He worked and lived on the Altyre estate with my grandad. He would preach the Gospel on a Sunday in a little church on the estate. Saturday nights would find him up at the Cross in Forres preaching to the passersby, namely those being ejected from the local pubs. He was a religious man all his life but I think my grandad had had enough of it because he was not a churchgoer, nor did he speak of the Bible in any way. I do think that my mother was influenced in a little way but that comes later.

Uncle Wilson (left) & friend

Both my uncles went to war, Charlie in 1943 and John in 1944. Both into Scottish regiments. Charlie was in the Lovat Scouts and John was in the Gordon Highlanders. They never got back home till after the war was two years finished. My Uncle Wilson was 10 years older than me so still a boy in those years. He and his good friend Lachie McCallum from up the road at the schoolhouse were very good to me, taking me with them when they went exploring.

I think our lives in the country were harder than those in the town, although I feel, much richer in quality. Our lives were governed by the seasons. Our winters were bitterly cold, snow piling upon snow. Sometimes it was so bad that Auntie Margaret and Uncle Wilson were walking along the top of the fence line to get to school, which was just a field away from the cottage. The school was called Half Davoch and the headmistress/teacher, Mrs McCallum, was Lachie's mother. She taught all ages from five years to 14 years. She was a well-respected and liked teacher and member of the community, who knew all her children and their families. If my father hadn't come home from the war sooner, I would have started my education there. Even years later, when I was a young teenager, she always spoke to me when we would meet in town.

Uncle Wilson, Granny Tough & Auntie Margaret

The winters were particularly hard for Auntie Margaret and Uncle Wilson because of the chores they had to do every morning. They had to get up quite early each morning, seven days a week, to walk up to McGillivray's farm to fetch the milk for the day. It was about two miles each way, up past the school towards the Romach Loch. There was a shortcut just at the school, cutting off the corner and through the woods but sometimes that would be impassable because of the snow. It was part of their day whether they liked it or not but they took it in turns.

Even on Christmas morning they still had to do it; but they always vied about who was to do it then because whoever did it got a slice of Christmas cake and a sixpence, a lot of money to a child in those days.

I must tell you about the water supply. I said earlier that we had a standpipe outside the cottage but in severe weather, the water could freeze and, so, Auntie Margaret had to go to the well down the road. It was about three hundred yards on a gentle slope down from the cottage, as the road turned sharply again to go up to the Davidsons, our nearest neighbours. To the right of the angle in the road there was a freshwater well. My granny always swore by it being fresher than the tap water.

Auntie Margaret had to take two big pails with her and a scoop. The scoop was used to get the water spiders out of the well. My granny always believed that if the spiders were in the well the water was pure. It seems to have worked, as no one took ill with it. I used to think I was helping Auntie Margaret by going to the well with her at times and I would take an end of a pail. She never said anything but I realize now that I must have been more of a hindrance than a help to her. I remember thinking what a long walk it was back up the road to the house carrying these pails, so I would have been about four years old. This would have been done a few times in a 24 hour period, hard work for a boy or girl and even for an adult, because we had to stop quite frequently to have a rest and put the pails down. This was all part of country life for us and I was amazed to see Granny Fraser had taps inside her house in Forres when I stayed there with my mam on weekends.

The winters could be quite cruel for us folks because we lived quite high above sea level and the frost was much harder up in the higher ground. There were compensations as far as the children were concerned. There was plenty of snow for sledging on homemade sledges, plenty of snowball fights, attempts at building igloos and, of course, the ice slides the boys made on the school playground and the road, with not a care for any poor cyclist who came upon one.

Obviously, I too had great fun in the snow. I was always well wrapped up for the cold. I remember that I had a bright red siren suit. This was an all-in-one suit with hood, gloves and feet as part of the garment. Under the hood I would wear a pixie. This was a hat that had a pointed top and tied under the chin. I would put a coat over my siren suit and little boots on my feet with socks underneath.

All winter long the frost hardly lifted and into the woods not far from grandad's sheds and chicken run there was a rough circular dip, quite big but only about four inches deep. Water collected there naturally over the years and it froze solid every winter. We had our own skating rink. After school the boys would charge across the road and into the wood to get to the rink, to have a slide before the fading daylight stopped the fun. Auntie Margaret and Uncle Wilson would take me there in the school holidays or when we couldn't get down to Forres because the road was blocked by snow. I just loved that rink. Auntie Margaret and Uncle Wilson would take a hand each and pull me along with them. Sometimes they would go off and have a slide by themselves, leaving me to try and slide on my own. I fell more times than I managed the knack of sliding and keeping my balance. Because I loved it so much, I never felt the cold, or the bumps on my backside, I was so well padded.

Those winters of the war were cold, hard and lean for many, both in town and country. But we had the advantage of having our fruit and vegetables from the garden preserved for the winters. There were rabbits to be caught in the fields; we had our own chickens, hens and fresh eggs, so we were okay as far as food went.

The big black range in the family room of the cottage had to be kept burning round the clock for warmth and cooking; there was no other means to heat the home. For lighting in the early years we had oil lamps but towards the end of the war we had paraffin Tilley lamps. For stoking the range we used firewood and occasionally peats *(blocks of peat harvested from bogs of peat)* to stock it at night to keep it in for the morning. My grandad was a woodsman by trade, so he knew which wood was best for burning and he was no stranger to a saw. Auntie Margaret and Uncle Wilson often had to take the other handle of the crosscut saw to saw the wood with grandad, as it made for a quicker, smoother action. This was no mean feat for children of nine and 12 respectively. Cutting and storing firewood was an ongoing job all year round because of the cooking and boiling of water for washing, etc.

THE food we ate was good and wholesome and I used to watch granny as she sat on the doorstep skinning and gutting rabbits, or plucking a hen that was too old to lay. Even today I could tell you how to prepare a rabbit for the pot having watched granny and mam do it over the years but I don't think I could bring myself to do it. There is one memory that sticks in my mind to this day. Grandad came over from the hen run with a cockerel that was getting too old. He'd wrung its neck before bringing it down to be plucked and hung it up on the porch wall on a nail, awaiting plucking and gutting. It was a huge black bird and I was fascinated by it just hanging head down above me. All of a sudden, it raised its head, like it was looking straight at me and let out this hellish crow and I immediately wet my knickers. They all thought it was hilarious, of course and I was screaming fit to bust. Seemingly this can happen but I am of the opinion that the cockerel had more of a hold on life than grandad gave him credit for. And, of course, he had to wring his neck all over again, poor thing, imagine being killed twice.

With the short daylight hours in the winter, the nights must have seemed very long, especially with just having oil lamps. There would always be knitting, ironing and mending to be done, all by this dim light. It must have been quite a strain on the eyes. And, of course, there would always be the men's pieces *(sandwiches)* to be prepared for their work next morning. There was no staying up late in granny's house; everyone went to bed early for they needed their sleep for the hard work they had to do each day.

A funny incident happened in the middle of one winter night. Even out in the country we still had wardens cycling around the neighbourhood, checking up that there were no lights showing in windows because of the blackout laws. There was a loud banging on the cottage door and granny had to get up to see what the racket was about. The warden was outside pointing up at the roof, shouting, "Get that light out, don't you know there's a war on?" Granny walked outside and looked up at where he was pointing, looked at him and said, "You silly auld goat, can't you see it's the moon reflecting off the skylight". He must have had a right red face when that got round the rurals.

Another funny incident happened with Auntie Margaret. She often came round to our room in Mrs McSteven's house after school to play a wee while with me. We were sitting on the floor playing a game. Auntie Margaret stood up and a mouse dropped out of her skirt. She hadn't felt it climb up her skirt and there was much screaming and dancing about the floor, the poor mouse could have had a heart attack.

My granny loved her flowers but I don't remember her ever cutting flowers from her garden. We always took home the wild flowers in season, which she would put in vases. One memory I have was in the springtime, when the larch trees look their loveliest in that glorious green, she would go out into the woods and pick a few little branches for her vases. They would have those beautiful deep pink 'roses' on them, which in the summer would turn to cones.

In the early autumn, just before harvest time, she would pick bunches of corn from the field at the back, for her winter vases. Each stalk of corn was separated at the seed head and the seed was wrapped in silver and gold foil. She must have painstakingly collected all these bits and pieces of foil over the years. It would have been an ongoing thing because she did it every harvest time. I used to watch her making her flower display, it was a slow process and it did take a lot of patience but she obviously enjoyed doing it.

Although spring was always that bit later coming to us, it was so welcome after the long winters. It was a pleasure to see green leaves on the trees again and, oh my, the spring wild flowers. There was a track that ran along the bottom of the two gardens and in a wide swathe, it took you down to the bottom of Annie Paul's brae, to where the Dava Way is now. Nearly down to the bottom of this track in the woods, Lily of the Valley grew in profusion. Auntie Margaret always took me down there in the spring to pick small bunches of them, one for granny and one for mam. Beautiful yellow primroses grew all down the bank of the glen too. The bank was to be found as you turned sharp left from the schoolhouse, down the steep hill, to the bridge over the Mosset burn, which ran across the bottom of the glen. This little glen was a favourite spot for all the school kids. It was just over the school wall. The nut trees were there to be climbed and the burn to be paddled in. I owe it to my then young aunt and uncle for the lovely memories that I still have of those days. Every spring I have these memories fresh again, when my own Lily of the Valley and primroses appear in my garden.

AT last the days were getting longer and I was allowed out to play across the road in grandad's wee wood. There was also a huge oak tree right across from the cottage, standing like a landmark on the very edge of the road. Its roots were exposed and there was fine golden sand in and around them. This was where I always played housies and tea parties with my dolls. I had two favourite stuffed animals, which I loved. They had been made for me by my Uncle Hugh, my dad's younger brother, whom I'd never met. The Red Cross had sent them on to me. My uncle was a prisoner of war in a stalag *(a German prisoner-of-war camp in World War II)*, somewhere in Germany. He must have got some felt from the Red Cross and made these lovely animals for me. Uncle Hugh was to be in that prisoner of war camp for four long years. His health was never the same after that. To all intents and purposes, they were starved in those camps. They had to eat grass in the end and I feel this is why he had a bad stomach for the rest of his life.

The summer was upon us once again and everyone was busy. Grandad was with his bee hives in the woods. I never went near them because I had been stung once in the garden and was terrified of them. Grandad received sugar from the government in the winter to keep the bees alive till they were making honey in the summer. Of course the bees got two-thirds of the sugar and my granny kept the other third

Grandad Tough

for making jam. We had the rasps and the blackcurrants to crop from the garden and the damsons from the tree. I was still helping Auntie Margaret cart the water from the well and I was getting better at it as I got older. There were some lovely wildflowers growing in the ditch where the water ran, they were quite tall with masses of mauve flowers. But Auntie Margaret wouldn't ever let me pick them because that would bring the thunder and lightning. I remember telling my own girls that when they were little. I still call them thunder flowers.

Chapter 2
1943-1945

Now that I was getting older, I was beginning to ask about my daddy, as to why he was never here. I knew about THE WAR but had no understanding of it. I knew that people wore uniforms, my Auntie Bess wore a strange one with trousers and I saw my two older uncles on one occasion wearing skirts, which my mother explained were kilts worn by Scottish soldiers. I saw a photo of my dad and he wore an even different uniform, as he was an able seaman, 1st class, in the Royal Navy. But my dad must have been in and out of my life in those years because my oldest brother Jimmy was born in April 1945. I have no memory of a baby in the family; my memory seems to be selective for that time in my life.

What I do remember are the happy days when school closed for summer and autumn and all the fun I had with Auntie Margaret, Uncle Wilson and sometimes Lachie McCallum. I remember a great adventure that Uncle Wilson and Lachie took me on. We were to go on a long walk to the head of the Loch of the Romach. It's about two miles there and two miles back, a long walk for me. I would have been about four at the time. Mam made us jammy pieces *(jam sandwiches)* and we had bottled water from the well. It was a hot day, as I remember and tiring. Once we were down in the glen, it was a gradual uphill walk, which took us well above the loch and then down again to the edge of the water. It was a long thin loch, very deep and we were heading for the opposite side. There were no trees on this side but great flat rocks that we climbed onto and lay down on. They were like tables because they were so flat and big. Just perfect for our picnic. That is one of my fondest memories.

When September came around, there was a lot of activity in the fields around us. The harvest had to be cut and the field next to our cottage was a great hive of activity with the farmers cutting the corn or barley. I used to watch them bind the sheaves and stook them *(sheaves set upright in a field to dry with their heads together)*. I would have great fun playing amongst them.

At this time, granny would take the chicks out of the hen run and lead theme across the road and into the field to eat the kernels of grain on the ground. When they had had their fill, she would lead them back again. It was quite funny to see them all marching along behind granny.

October was a great time of year for foraging. There were hazelnuts to be gathered in the glen and brambles to be picked in the hedges and woods. Also, there were so many blaeberries *(blueberries)* to be found in the woods too. They seem to like growing around heather. They grew so low to the ground that it was easy for me to pick them but hard on your back if you were taller. Granny made loads of jam then with the wild berries. There was no other way to preserve them in those days. And so we lived our lives by the seasons, each season bringing more delights to my childish eyes. I couldn't have known then that I'd have these memories to remember all my life.

DURING those years we never lacked for news from the town. Thompson the grocer came round every week, as did Forrest the baker and McKenzie and Cruickshank with methylated spirits for our lamps. It was a great way for the grown-ups to get all the gossip and scandal from the town and round the rurals and, sadly, whose son had been lost in the war.

As well as my life in the country, I also had my life with my other granny and grandad, my Fraser family in Forres. Every weekend, my Granny Tough had a taxi on order to take us down to Forres town for the messages. That's what everyone called shopping in those days.

There was a taxi driver in town called Fat Bobs and he used to come up to Craigroy to collect us every Saturday morning. And he was fat. It took him all his time to get in and out of the car. He had four chins and was always smiling and jovial. He knew everyone and everybody knew him. He had a huge black car and Granny Tough would sit in the front, dressed up in her good clothes and she always wore a hat. She was very formal on these occasions. Mam sat in the back with me on her knee, Uncle Wilson and Auntie Margaret beside us and we'd drive down to town in style. That was before Jimmy was born. He would be the one sitting on mam's knee then and still room to spare in the back. Granny and Grandad Fraser's house seemed amazingly big to me. They lived at the top of St Ronans Road, in Forres. They even

Grandad Fraser, Granny Fraser, Me *(Violet)*, Mum, Maggie, Jenks & Davy

had a cooker that worked with gas. The house also had gaslights, which worked by lighting a mantle and, wonder of wonders, an inside toilet that flushed. There was even a bath with taps that ran hot water.

Grandad Fraser was a salmon fisher on the river Findhorn in the season and worked on a farm the rest of the year. He worked all year round, never taking a break. I don't think he would have known how to deal with free time. He was a quiet man, with very little to say.

While the rest of the family went shopping mam took me round to my Granny Fraser's. There, we would spend the weekend. Mam would catch up with all the news in the family and I would be thoroughly spoilt by Granny and Grandad Fraser and their other children, Uncle Davy, Auntie Maggie and Auntie Connie. Uncle Davy and Uncle Wilson would be about the same age, Auntie Maggie a couple of years older with the eldest being Auntie Connie who was a couple of years older again. I remember Auntie Maggie taking me into the bath with her at Granny Fraser's house and I thought it was marvellous just to pull out the plug and the water disappeared.

Auntie Connie was engaged to marry a French Canadian called Vian, who was based in Forres during the war. He used to be at the house sometimes and I had great fun with him when he used to chase me on his hands and knees around granny's table legs, causing plenty

Auntie Connie & Mum (*Jean*)

of giggles.

Sometimes mum would go out at night with them to see friends or go to a dance. I did not like that at all. I remember screaming the house down when mam left me with Granny Fraser. But apart from that I did love it down at Forres. Davy and his pal Jenks would take me up to Grant Park, less than a five minute walk from the house. I loved this park, ringed with trees and Cluny Hill rising up from the back of it. We would usually take a ball with us and play catch or football.

I DO remember a time when Grandad Fraser took Jimmy and me, along with dad down to the river to see his boat one Sunday. Jimmy and I were all dressed up in our Sunday best for an outing with Grandad Fraser. He intended to take us all out for a row on the river. Jimmy and I were put in the boat first then dad. Grandad was just getting into the boat when the river came down like a mini tidal wave. It was a flash flood and it was instant. Grandad barely managed to get us out before the boat was swamped. That was really scary. I would have been about five and Jimmy about two years old.

Granny Fraser was a kind and loving woman, whose life revolved around her family. When she got the news that her son, Uncle Hugh, had been captured and was in a prisoner of war camp, we believed she never came out of her house again. Even after the war had ended and Uncle Hugh was repatriated, she stayed within her house for the rest of her life. She saw that the young boy who had gone to do his duty by his country had come home a much changed and quiet man, whose ill health, due to the treatment in the prisoner of war camp, was to last his lifetime. *(We were led to believe that granny had never left home again, but years later we learned from my sister Jean that Uncle Hugh had bought a car and took Granny Fraser out for runs at weekends. We never saw the car so we have no idea where he kept it!)*

My dad, who was the eldest of the Fraser family, came back safe and sound in body but would never talk about the war. He would tell us kids when pressed about the countries he'd been to but that was all. I learned more in my adult years from my Uncle John Tough, who told me that dad had operated the radio machine in the submarines that detected depth charges. When working on destroyers, he was on convoys to Murmansk, Russia. They sailed out of Scotland to

Murmansk to give the Russians ammunition to help fight the war. I know through my own reading about the war on the high seas that so many young men died on the convoys. (*"Torpedo boat destroyers, destroyers, or (slang) tin cans served all of the major sea powers well during WWII. They were the smallest, general purpose, ocean-going warships of the various blue water fleets and they often took heavy losses in action. That was perhaps inevitable, as destroyers were employed in many roles besides hunting torpedo boats and submarines, their original purposes.*

Destroyers were used to lay minefields outside of enemy harbours and to transport troops and supplies to beleaguered outposts in enemy controlled waters that were too dangerous for conventional transports to negotiate. They escorted convoys, provided air and gunfire support for larger and more vulnerable ships (such as troop transports and aircraft carriers), attacked superior enemy forces, bombarded invasion beaches well within the range of enemy shore batteries, scouted for their fleets and served as radar pickets far from the protection of friendly naval forces. They were expected to put themselves at risk to protect their charges, whether merchant ships or heavy warships. Destroyers fought submarines, aircraft and surface actions against all other classes of warships, from battleships to MTB's (Motor Torpedo Boats). Destroyers occasionally operated alone, but more often they were formed into flotillas or squadrons, which would then jointly be assigned a task, such as to escort a convoy, screen a task force, or to attack an enemy surface force with torpedoes and gunfire.

Destroyers of all the major sea powers were lost during the war in the course of what were essentially suicide charges at far more powerful enemy surface ships. The courage and dedication of destroyer men clearly transcended national boundaries. Destroyers were viewed as expendable ships in both world wars and many of their brave crews paid the ultimate price." - The Best Destroyers of World War II, by Chuck Hawks.)

AS I said before, Saturdays were the days when all the country folk, farmers with their wives, farm workers, young men and women not yet of an age to be called up to fight, came into Forres from all the nearby villages and hamlets. The men, young and old would gather on street corners to discuss cattle and crops; the young men watching the young girls go by and probably telling each other which of the forces they hoped to join when their turn came to go and fight for their country. The women of the family would be meeting in the shops and exchanging gossip. The older kids would be keeping an eye on the younger ones, probably taking them to the rose gardens or up to the needle monument to play with the other kids.

It was a grand day out, away from the cares of home and everyone made the most of it. In those days, Forres was a thriving town with over 60 shops on or just off the high street. There was never any need to go to any other town for there was everything to be had right there.

Granny Tough had her own set of shops that she supported. There was Forrest the baker, where Ashers is now and, across the road, there was Fish Jess, which is the Thistle Bar now. Along by the town clock she would do her grocery shopping at Thomsons and next door was Fraser the butcher. Of course there were long queues because of food rationing but that didn't bother the womenfolk, as it gave them more time to chat.

This was where my dad trained to be a butcher. When he was 14, he left school and learned this skill at Frasers. He became fully qualified and then he was 'called up' and joined the Navy. While he was doing his National Service, war broke out *(WWII)*. After the war he couldn't face going back to being a butcher because of the images he saw during the war. *(Conscription to military service was a system whereby the state required all men - and in a few cases women - to serve a period in the armed forces. The British government introduced National Service in 1938. All men aged between 18 and 41 were 'called up' and had to register with the government. Government officials then decided whether they should go into the army or do other war work. Most young men were recruited into the armed forces. This created a severe labour shortage and on 18th December 1941, the National Service Act was passed by Parliament. This legislation called up unmarried women aged between twenty and thirty. Later this was extended to married women, although pregnant women and mothers with young children were exempt from this work. – Spartacus Educational.)*

One vital need was for women to work in munitions factories. Other women were conscripted to work in tank and aircraft factories, civil defence, nursing, transport and other key occupations. This involved jobs that had been traditionally seen as 'men's work' such as driving trains and operating anti-aircraft guns.

In the afternoon the womenfolk would retire to the Forres tearooms, which were situated on the High Street directly opposite the top of Cumming Street. Here they would have afternoon tea, consisting of whatever the kitchen staff could get their hands on to make sandwiches, cakes and scones. The younger element would go to Zandre's for ice cream and probably a flirt with the boys. In the evening the men would retire to the local pubs and the women and kids would get a chance to go to the pictures, which was where Whites Removers now have their offices. And of course there was always a dance in the Drill Hall for the young girls and young men of every nationality, with so many air force camps around Forres. One camp was called RAF Forres, which was based at Kinloss. At Mundole there was another airfield. There were also Canadian lumberjacks who were based on the Darnaway estate. These men built the Bailey bridge for quick access. There were Polish pilots who were trained for the D-Day landings, American pilots and various other escapees from Europe and they all attended the dances in the Drill Hall. Of course, there were always a few sair heidies *(sore heads)* the next morning but it was get up and get on with it, regardless.

Chapter 3
1946

In January of this year my Grandad Tough sadly died of stomach cancer. My mother took me to see him for the last time in hospital. I didn't understand quite what it meant to die, although I was told he was going to Heaven. To my lifelong shame, all I could think about at his bedside was an orange sitting in a glass bowl by his bed. I had never eaten an orange or even tasted one. Although the war had been over in Europe for nearly a year, things like oranges and bananas were almost impossible to come by. I remember kicking and screaming by his bed, shouting for his orange and my grandad saying to mam, "Gie the quine it." (*"Give it to the girl"*). That was the last time I heard my grandad speak. It still saddens and shames me after all these years to think that this is the outstanding memory I have of Grandad Tough.

My dad still had not been demobbed (*released*) from the Royal Navy. I would be four years old in April, with another wonderful spring and summer to look forward to up at Craigroy cottage. My baby brother Jimmy would also be one year old in April, although I still have no memory of a baby in the family. I find it strange to this day, because I can recall so much of what was going on in my life in those years. Maybe it was sibling jealousy on my part because I had been so spoilt and just blocked out certain memories. Who knows?

This year was to be a good, happy year for all of us. My Uncle Hugh was released from the prisoner of war camp and came home to the family at last. My dad came home, finally, for good. He had been offered promotion to Petty Officer if he would like to make a career in the navy. Mam said no, she'd missed him too much over the long years of the war. He too had had enough of it. Eight years was too long, he just wanted to have a family life at long last. That was in August and we had to find somewhere to live because my uncles would be coming home too, sooner or later.

Although World War II was finally over, many of the men had not come back yet. There were still skirmishes ongoing, people like the Jews had to be protected, cities were in ruins and people starving. Many of the allied soldiers had to keep the lawlessness from getting out of hand. For many of the families waiting at home it was a fraught, worrying time and they were longing to see their sons, brothers and husbands home for good at last.

There were many scenes of joy, anguish and sorrow at our little railway station in Forres. In those far off days you could get on a train in London and it would take you straight up the country, through all those miles to our little station without a single change. It stopped at all the little towns and country stations. Soldiers whose homes were out in the country would get off, say at Dunphail, if they lived around there and would shoulder their kitbags and walk the last couple of miles, probably savouring the wonderful scent of their own country air. For all of those men, it might have been a time of reflection as they neared home, maybe a time to say a little prayer of thankfulness that they had survived, while others perished. Sorrow for childhood friends they might never see again, the boys who didn't make it back. Some of those men came home whole in body but affected forever by the horrors of war, others came back who were the walking wounded. Some just made it home to die. So amongst all the flag waving and rejoicing, there was also the mourning for those lost forever in some foreign field, or buried in a strange land. Many countries would continue to honour them as the years would go by. One of my mother's stories, which I remember was of a local man whose name I cannot remember, who made it through the war and travelled home only to die on his doorstep, probably from the strain of the war and the hardships our men and women endured at that time.

Mum (*Jean*) & Me (*Violet*)

Chapter 4
1947

In late 1946 we finally made the move to Forres. My dad had found us a small house right at the bottom of Gordon Street. It was a tiny cottage which sat in its own big garden. The front door opened onto the pavement and it was opposite the laundry house. In front of the garden was a large shed opening onto the opposite pavement from us, which I think was McLean's cycle repair shop. Just slightly up Gordon Street hill, the McLean family had their house in its own garden. It was a lovely old house with green pillars at the front and it was enclosed by a high stone wall from the pavement. All the houses leading up Gordon Street had their front doors onto the pavement leading up to the High Street, as they still do today. Down at the bottom of the street, as I said, was our house. Crossing the roadside on to our house at the bottom of North Road was a little shop on the corner. Then along the road on the right, towards Tesco's old shop, those little houses still remain the same as they were all those years ago.

The other side of the road was totally different in those days. There was the laundry where the Mosset Tavern sits today and the duck pond was the drying green for the laundry. I remember on sunny days watching the rows of sheets flapping and snapping in the wind. There was also a small underground stream that ran from behind the laundry and surfaced just in front of it. It widened quickly as it came to the surface and ran alongside the road towards the bridge opposite the old Tesco building and it then ran into the Mosset Burn. This stream we called the Laundry Burn. It was quite wide, about six or seven feet and I was always paddling in it. It was only shallow; maybe six to nine inches deep, so my mam was never worried about me playing there.

There were not many children of my age living around us because there was no housing for all the young families after the war. It was quite a lonely time. It was also very strange to be living in a town.

There was no open countryside to play in and I missed my aunt and uncle very much. But they all still came down to town every Saturday and visited us. My older uncles, home from the war, used to leave their bikes at our house on Saturday nights, when they came into town to the dances.

By this time my dad was working at The Bobbin Mill (*Flemington's*), which was situated down by the Mechanics football ground. Quite a few of the returning young men found work there and also at Bremners sawmill, which was in the town as well. There were lots of sawmills around Forres, luckily for the young men, as there were no other jobs at that time. It was the same all over Scotland.

I had a little girlfriend by then and we used to play housies together (*pretending to cook and clean, etc*). One day we were in our usual spot behind some sheds playing and this boy appeared. I'd seen him around before, he was about 14 or 15 years old and always wore dungarees. He asked what were we doing and we said, "Playing housies".

He asked us if we would like to play another game but I don't remember us replying. He then said we had to take off our knickers to play this game. I didn't reply, just hung my head. I felt like I couldn't move, I was so scared. I didn't know what I was scared of but knew it wasn't right. I wouldn't look at him, just at his feet standing in front of me. I don't know how long I stood like that, it felt like forever and then I suddenly bolted from behind the shed and ran home. I didn't tell mam or dad about this because I was scared, of what I didn't know.

MANY years later, I was walking along the High Street after collecting my oldest daughter from Andersons School and pushing my youngest in the push chair, when I heard someone call out, "Hallo Violet" and looked round about to see who it was. Across the street in front of the town hall, a man was smiling at me. I recognized him instantly as the boy in the dungarees and I just felt sick. How he knew me I'll never know and here was me with my own little girl of six years. I never saw him again after the incident when I was a girl, so assumed he was only on holiday. But for a long time after that, I always collected my daughter from school.

When I was a young woman, I was a victim of sexual harassment at work. I told my mother about it from the start but she didn't know what to do, or how to advise me. I asked her not to tell dad, I felt ashamed. I could not give up my job because I needed to earn money. I decided all I could do was never be alone with the man who was harassing me, ever. I tried to make sure that there were always people around me. He would often try to give me gifts, which I refused and I ignored the sexual innuendoes directed at me. All I could hope was that he got the message. It all ended when he had a change of circumstances, so I was free to get on with my life without that hanging over me.

Groom Tom, bride Auntie Bess, bridesmaid, Auntie Margaret & Me (*Violet*)

In April of this year, 1947, my sister Jean was born. In that month Jimmy was two years old and I was five years old. I was to go to school in the August of that year. I was not looking forward to it. I still hadn't met many children and my life revolved around my family and home. Mam took me up to see the Forres Primary School and I was not impressed, it looked so old and forbidding. There was a back entrance at the top of North Road, which I would use because the road from our little house ran straight up to the gate. There was a front entrance at the other side, which led directly onto the East End of the High Street. There were playgrounds from front to back and huge old trees around the edges and three entrances. Infants were at the back, juniors in the middle and seniors at the front. We never mixed, always staying in our own part of the playground. The toilets were a separate building, set in the grounds and even now I shudder when I think of them. They were dark and dank and scary and I hated the thought of using them. The dreaded day came and mam walked me to school and put me in the gate. Mothers were definitely not encouraged to stay. We were herded like sheep, told to do this, do that, stand there and come when your name is called. We were all totally bewildered, the teachers were so old and scary and they shouted all the time. We were finally shown to our classrooms and we were allocated a desk each. We were told we would sit there for the year. And so my little hell on earth began. Our teacher was old with tight grey hair and she walked around us with a long wooden pointer stick, which she kept whacking on the desks at the least provocation. I think those old biddies of long ago thought that the louder they shouted and flailed their sticks around, the quicker we would learn. It was not uncommon for children to wet themselves, too scared to ask to go to the toilet and that made things worse. And so my school life began.

I hated school but I was in for a bit of relief from it. My Auntie Bess was married that winter and I was the flower girl. I was not feeling well on the wedding day but things went ahead, mam thinking it was a bit of excitement but she was wrong. The Monday after I went to school as usual and the school nurse was there to examine us. She looked at me and thought that I had scarlet fever, so she took me home and told mam to get the doctor straight away. Once he examined me and confirmed that I did in fact have scarlet fever, I was taken to the fever hospital at Spiny in Elgin. I was in there for a long time. When I first went in I was horrified to see I was the only child in a ward full of men. I used to hide under the blankets most of the time and sing to myself. The weeks passed in a dream. Mam couldn't bring me anything in to play with because everything would be burned. Toys and books were not easy to come by in those days so it would have been a shame for them to be destroyed.

CHRISTMAS finally arrived. I was so miserable because I was still ill and couldn't go home. Mam brought me the loveliest cake I'd ever seen. It was fully iced and decorated for Christmas and the Sister carried it in to the ward in style, showing it to all the men. Then she took it away again. She cut it all up and gave the entire ward a slice, which they all enjoyed, except me. I was so angry - it was MY cake. Sister refused to let me have a piece. I'm not sure why, she never told me but there must have been a reason. I sulked for days after.

On Christmas Eve night the ward lights were dimmed and the nurses came in carrying candles and singing carols, it was really lovely. Then they all asked me if I would sing for them. I realised that they must have been listening to me singing under the covers. The only hymn I could remember was *Away in a Manger.*

I didn't get out of hospital until January 1948. My Christmas presents were waiting for me at home and all my family came to see me. We had a lovely time and I was so happy to be home at last.

I had been back at school for a few weeks and still hating it, when I had an accident at home. Dad and I were playing a board game, both of us sitting on the floor by the fire. It was one of these old fashioned fireplaces that had a shelf attached to the front of it. Mam had a big black kettle sitting on it full of simmering water. In my excitement with the game, I kicked out with my foot and knocked the kettle off the shelf and all the boiling water went over my leg and thigh. All I can remember is dad pulling off my woolly stockings and the excruciating pain.That was another stay in hospital for me. When I did get home, the doctor or nurse had to come by every day to change the dressings

Mum (*Jean*) Dad (*James*) Me (*Violet*) & Jimmy (*brother*)

and clart *(smear)* stinky brown goo on the burns. The smell was terrible but that's what they did for burns in those days. The burn covered a large area, from my knee to the top of my ankle and up to my thigh. It took a long time to heal and grow new skin so I was off school for another few weeks, which didn't bother me at all. But I had an awful lot of catching up to do when I did go back.

By this time it was late spring and there were only a couple of months more of school and it would be the summer holidays. I had been off so much that I didn't get to know my classmates, so in the second year it would be like starting over again with strangers. Also, the summer months were to bring more changes in my life.

C.IX.—No. 5116. Registered at the General Post Office as a Newspaper. **FORRES, W**

SQUATTERS AT BALNAGEITH

Department's Proposal to County Council

Sanitary Conditions "None Too Good"

Moray County Council have been asked by the Department of Health if they are prepared to take over and manage squatters' huts at Balnageith Camp, Forres.

The matter was discussed at a meeting of Moray County Council on Monday — Col. Grant Peterkin, Grangehall, presiding. The following letter from the De-

"ROUND THE RURALS"

FINDHORN.— The first meeting of the winter session of Findhorn

Forres, Elgin & Nairn Gazette
22nd October 1947
Courtesy of Scottish Provincial Press

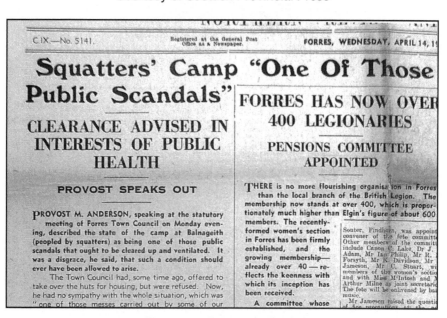

C.IX.—No. 5141. Registered at the General Post Office as a Newspaper. **FORRES, WEDNESDAY, APRIL 14, 1**

Squatters' Camp "One Of Those Public Scandals"

CLEARANCE ADVISED IN INTERESTS OF PUBLIC HEALTH

PROVOST SPEAKS OUT

PROVOST M. ANDERSON, speaking at the statutory meeting of Forres Town Council on Monday evening, described the state of the camp at Balnageith (peopled by squatters) as being one of those public scandals that ought to be cleared up and ventilated. It was a disgrace, he said, that such a condition should ever have been allowed to arise.

The Town Council had, some time ago, offered to take over the huts for housing, but were refused. Now, he had no sympathy with the whole situation, which was "one of those messes carried out by some of our

FORRES HAS NOW OVER 400 LEGIONARIES

PENSIONS COMMITTEE APPOINTED

THERE is no more flourishing organisation in Forres than the local branch of the British Legion. The membership now stands at over 400, which is proportionately much higher than Elgin's figure of about 600 members. The recently-formed women's section in Forres has been firmly established, and the growing membership — already over 40 — reflects the keenness with which its inception has been received.

A committee whose

Souter, Findhorn, was appoint convener of the fete committ Other members of the commit include Canon C. Lake, Dr J. Adam, Mr Ian Philip, Mr R. Forsyth, Mr K. Davidson, Mr Jameson, Mr C. Stuart, wi members of the women's sect and with Miss M'Intosh and Arthur Milne as joint secretari The fete will be enlivened by ba music.

Mr Jameson raised the questi of fire precautions at the

Forres, Elgin & Nairn Gazette
14th April 1948
Courtesy of Scottish Provincial Press

Chapter 5
1947-1948

My mam told me that we had to move out of our little house because she had seen a rat in our bedroom and we just couldn't stay there anymore. The Council wouldn't do anything about it and they couldn't house us because there were no houses being built and no pre-war houses to let. Everybody was looking for a house or flat. All the young families, reunited after the war, were desperate for somewhere to live and be a proper family again. My mam told me we were going to the 'huts' to live and I had no idea what she meant. My uncles helped us to flit *(move)* and dad and I were the last to go. He took me on the crossbar of his racer bike and it seemed to take forever to get to this place where we were to live.

It was called the Burdshaugh camp, in the countryside on the edge of the town, where MacDonald Drive is today. The layout of the drive follows the layout of the huts. There were a circle of huts with a central hut and a toilet block. The road ran, as it does today, up the short hill and round inside the buildings in a circle and out again to meet the road going down. On two sides of the site were the Sanquhar woods, a field with the railway running alongside and the houses at Fleurs Place at the bottom of the hill. I had never seen anything like this and I was quite intrigued by it all. I saw that there were a lot of people about and children too. I was pleased about this - I would have kids to play with.

My mam and dad had chosen the middle hut and, when I went in, I was amazed to see how big it was. There was a stove set in the middle and that was it. No dividing walls, just one huge area. Mam told me that we would be sharing this hut with another family, called Helen and Paul and baby Paul. Mam and Helen were to become lifelong friends.

Uncle Hugh had married and he and my new Auntie Margaret *(who we all called 'Auntie Margaret, Hugh's wife' to differentiate from my Auntie Margaret, mum's sister)* had also moved into a hut and he built walls inside, partitioning the area to make a proper living space. I was told that there were other relations living here whom I would meet once we settled in. It all seemed quite bewildering to me. First I lived in the country and then I lived in the town. Now I'd be living in between in a hut. I didn't quite know what to make of it.

There were a lot of prisoner of war camps all over the UK. They were transit camps for Germans and Poles. Some of these Polish Army camps were set out down the western boundaries of Forres. The Poles as prisoners of war were in the camps briefly before they were moved elsewhere. There was the Sanquhar camp, Burdshaugh camp, Balnaferry camp, Balnageith camp, Thornhill camp, Whiterow camp and Waterford camp. When the prisoners of war were repatriated to their own countries and the Polish Army moved out, the huts on these camps were left empty. However, many Poles, who were unable to return home because of boundary changes, stayed and moved into these huts too. Young families with nowhere to live decided to move into these huts until houses were built for them. Neither the local council nor the County Council could stop this happening as they had no alternative to offer them.

There were so many families with nowhere to live. But there were also people coming up from the south of Scotland looking for somewhere to live and they were looking at these empty huts too.

Articles were printed in the old Forres newspapers, which said that many of these homeless people were 'undesirables'. Some of the local people of Forres cast us all to be the same. We were called the 'squatters' and this became the dirty word used for us. They did not seem to care that so many of us were local people with husbands and fathers who fought in the very recent war. These men had fought to

8.   With which is incorporated the "Strathspey and Badenoch Times."   PRICE THREE HALFPENCE

HUT DWELLERS DISTRESSED BY COUNCIL REPORTS

ACCOMMODATION AT CAMP PRAISED

LAST week it was reported what was said by the chair at the statutory meeting of Forres Town Council with regard to the condition of the squatters' camp at Balnageith. Some of the statements made are greatly resented by the 22 inhabitants of the technical site (i.e. the group of buildings in close vicinity of Balnageith House, and on that side of the public roadway).

So distressed are these people by the general picture suggested to the Council that the " Gazette " was approached to publish their side of the matter, and interviews made on the camp site by a representative of this newspaper are printed below.

Mrs C. Renouf, wife of an R.A.F.

WEATHER IN MARCH

MONTH OF RECORDS

FORRES and Nairn had each 1 hours of sunshine last mont which was the warmest March f a great many years. All kinds records have been set up by th weather within the past few we —good and bad, from the people point of view—and this is furthe shown by the fact that only tw Marchs in the last century had higher mean temperature tha last month.

The opening week of the mont was cool and fair, then after few days of wet, unsettled weath warm southerly breezes gave short dry and sunny spell (b tween the 9th and 14th). Cool conditions persisted till the 21s but the next seven days wer brilliantly bright and summe like, with shade temperature rising to 65-70 degrees in all di

Forres, Elgin & Nairn Gazette
21st April 1948
Courtesy of Scottish Provincial Press

free millions of people from monstrous prejudices, only to come up against it in their own home town.

I never knew how my parents handled this, for they never spoke of it within my hearing and I never ever told them about how we were treated or the name calling that went on at school and in the town. The children in our huts stayed close together as a group for protection from the town children and the older boys could always be relied upon to help us if we were ganged up on.

There were two gangs in those days, the Bogton Road Gang and the Huts Gang. My Uncle John told me that there were violent confrontations in those days, hard to believe in Forres. I do remember that we had built a huge bonfire in preparation for Guy Fawkes Night on the 5th November. The night before, the Bogton Roaders sneaked in and lit it. It's quite amusing looking back on it but it just kept the 'warfare' going.

We were a very mixed bunch of people on our site and it was the same on other sites. I came to know a few of the residents quite well. Best of all, there were two girls of my age who were to become good friends and their brother James who was a bit older than us. They were Anna and Joan Watson. There were also my dad's cousins - Hughie Miller and his sisters - and their mother, an RAF officer and his wife, who were to become good friends with my parents and Helen and Paul next door to us. Helen was a cook in the Carlton Hotel; Paul was a Free Pole in the Polish Army. There was the Murray family who had goats, which I found very interesting, the McMannis and the McQueen families, whose children were a bit older than me. Cathy McQueen was to become a very dear friend of mine in later years when we met up again in Germany. Our friendship continued throughout our lives until she was murdered in her home on New Year's morning 20 years ago. She was murdered simply because she took pity on her murderer. Cathy was a nurse in Craig Dunain House Hospital in Inverness. She loved her work and was highly thought of by both patients and staff. She was always helping someone, well over and above what was expected of her. Taking pity on all 'lame dogs' was the reason she died in the end. Hogmanay 1992 Cathy took into her home two young men who had finished treatment at the hospital but had nowhere to go. Between midnight and 10am the following morning, one of the young men shot her in the head for no apparent reason. They were each given eight years custodial sentence.

1948 saw two new births in the Fraser families - my second brother David; and my first cousin Sheila was born to Uncle Hugh and Auntie Margaret, Hugh's wife. I have often wondered how Uncle Hugh could come to terms with having to live in a hut inside a camp, which must have reminded him daily of his four years in a prisoner of war camp. The men in the families must have felt very much let down by their town and Council.

Chapter 6
1948-1949

I did a lot of researching for this book in the back numbers of the *Forres, Elgin & Nairn Gazette* and I was shocked to read about what was said about us 'squatters'. It seems that the County Council, in whose area the huts were in, was asked by government bodies to take over and rehouse us in the course of time. They refused to do this and asked the Burgh Council to take the huts over, which they refused to do. They said some of the squatters were problem families and not welcome. Later, Forres Town Council wanted permission to build a new housing scheme but were told they would only get permission if they rehoused the squatters. They finally did so and had the cheek to say that 'the squatters fitted in admirably'.

While all this toing and froing was going on there was an 'Anti-Squatter Brigade' formed by the current tenants of Roysvale. Shades of vigilantism here. They got up a petition to try to stop us moving into the houses. Fortunately nothing came of it and we were allowed to move in.

A company of Polish Army soldiers who were occupying a prisoner of war camp in Banff were sent by the local council to occupy the huts at Balnageith. This was to make sure that no squatters could live in the empty huts and this was welcomed by the townsfolk. It seems to me that some people of the town took their lead from the Council and treated all homeless people like intruders who had no right to be in their town. It was very upsetting because a lot of us were Forres born and bred.

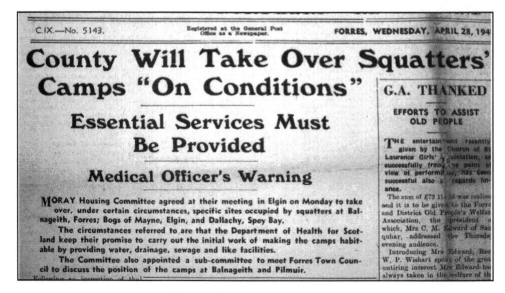

C.IX.—No. 5143. Registered at the General Post Office as a Newspaper. FORRES, WEDNESDAY, APRIL 28, 194

County Will Take Over Squatters' Camps "On Conditions"

Essential Services Must Be Provided

Medical Officer's Warning

MORAY Housing Committee agreed at their meeting in Elgin on Monday to take over, under certain circumstances, specific sites occupied by squatters at Balnageith, Forres; Bogs of Mayne, Elgin, and Dallachy, Spey Bay.

The circumstances referred to are that the Department of Health for Scotland keep their promise to carry out the initial work of making the camps habitable by providing water, drainage, sewage and like facilities.

The Committee also appointed a sub-committee to meet Forres Town Council to discuss the position of the camps at Balnageith and Pilmuir.

G.A. THANKED

EFFORTS TO ASSIST OLD PEOPLE

THE entertainment recently given by the Church of St Laurence Girls' Association, successfully from the point of view of performance, has been successful also as regards finance.

The sum of £72 11s 6d was realised and it is to be given to the Forres and District Old People's Welfare Association, the president of which, Mrs C. M. Edward of Sanquhar, addressed the Thursday evening audience.

Introducing Mrs Edward, Rev W. P. Wishart spoke of the great untiring interest Mrs Edward has always taken in the welfare of th

Forres, Elgin & Nairn Gazette
28 April 1948
Courtesy of Scottish Provincial Press

I had no idea that this conflict was going on during the time I lived at the Burdshaugh huts as a child. I was living in my own small world and this only included my new friends and my family.

We all went together to school each day and it was a long walk for little kids, from the top of MacDonald Drive down to where the community centre is today and back in the afternoon. School was a different experience for me now, I felt that I was not the same as them and I even felt this uncomfortable feeling coming from the teachers as well. The name-calling started in the playground and continued in whispers in the classroom, all done by the boys mostly. I was the only one in my class from the huts because Joan and Anna were in different classrooms. They were lucky because they had James to look out for them. None of us liked the long walk home after school. We never knew what kids would be lying in wait for us to call us names and make fun of us. We walked mostly with our heads down so as to avoid meeting anyone's eyes. I felt that I'd done something wrong and the whole town knew about it but no one would tell me what. Of course town children took their lead from their parents, so we just suffered in silence. The boys from the huts, being boys, would fight back, stand up for themselves but we girls never did and we just stayed within the camp boundaries.

Even though all of this taunting was going on, we had a lot of fun in those years, climbing trees, exploring Sanquhar Woods and the pond, which was a full pond then. Mrs Edwards, who owned the estate, was a lovely woman, a true gentlewoman, who allowed us kids to wander in her woods as long as we did no damage. She sometimes would stop and speak to the women of the huts while out for a walk. Every Halloween she came to the huts with her butler and dogs with baskets of apples from her orchards for the kids. She was very well liked and respected by all of us.

Between the western boundary of our camp and the railway line was a big field belonging to a farmer called Scott, who actually had his farm in the town, along the burn where the flats and the health centre are today. The bridge over the burn has always been known as 'Scotties Bridge'.

Sanquhar House
Courtesy of Raymond Mills

C.IX.—No. 5147.   Registered at the General Post Office as a Newspaper.   FORRES, WE

SQUATTERS TO BE OFFERED OTHER ACCOMMODATION

DIED IN CLASSROOM

FORMER FORRES TEACHER

A FORMER member of the staff of Forres Academy, Mr George Adam, collapsed and died just after 9 o'clock yesterday morning in a classroom at Duffus Junior Secondary School, Hopeman, of which he was headmaster.

Mr Adam left Forres 21 years ago (1927) to take up

HUTS WILL BE MADE UNINHABITABLE

SUGGESTED INCREASE IN CHARGES

THE squatters now occupying the huts on the Balnageith site of the R.A.F.'s former aerodrome at Forres are to be given alternative accommodation on sites at Sanquhar and Fleurs. This was decided by a joint meeting in Forres on Friday of representatives of the Public Health Committees of Moray County Council and Forres Town Council.

It was stated that at the Sanquhar and Fleurs sites

Forres, Elgin & Nairn Gazette
26 May 1948
Courtesy of Scottish Provincial Press

There was always something of interest going on in this field, from the plowing and planting to the harvesting. It was always a grain field and at harvest time it was great just to watch the men cut the corn, tie it together and build the stooks. The rabbits and field mice would be running all over the place. The men were a cheery bunch and always spoke to us and made us laugh with their jokes. Scottie would always warn us of dire consequences if we were to play among the stooks when they were finished with the harvest. Of course we always played amongst them when he was gone. What child could resist playing housies or hide and seek in the field. We had great fun for weeks on end. We played the same games when the corn was high as well - he was always chasing us off the field with some ripe language.

Across the field on the boundary was the railway line and we got to know when a train was due and we used to run across the field and wait at the boundary fence to wave to the people on the train, who always waved back. We could hear it in the distance as it came thundering down the hill from Dunphail and under the bridge at Mannachie, throwing great gouts of smoke from its chimney. The driver would blow his horn as he neared Forres. We used to say to each other that we would be the passengers on that train one day, coming home from some fantastic place to see our town again. We had our dreams like all kids do, of mystical faraway places we wanted to see one day.

Forres, Elgin & Nairn Gazette
June 1948
Courtesy of Scottish Provincial Press

Forres, Elgin & Nairn Gazette
1st September 1948
Courtesy of Scottish Provincial Press

Exterior of derelict hut at Balnageith 2012

Interior of derelict hut at Balnageith 2012. Block walls were constructed inside to partition it off into two family units. Evidence of the block wall partitions can be seen between the windows. The huts had single skin brick walls with no insulation
Courtesy of Peter Jones

Chapter 7
1949

By the end of 1948 all the huts on our camp were occupied. Just behind the trees from us were the Sanquhar huts, where Mannachie Terrace is now and it was full too. People were desperate for somewhere to live and the Council had nothing to give them. Eventually, it was decided that they would take responsibility and partition off the huts into two family units. The Council built a breeze block wall across the middle of the huts, then block walls to divide the space into two bedrooms. At least we all had a degree of privacy. I even remember mam trying to hang wallpaper. She also started a small flower garden. Mam and dad were both still young and optimistic and they were determined to give us a family life despite living under these conditions. There were many families now living in the Thornhill huts and the Polish Army were billeted at the Balnageith and Waterford camps. They were well thought of in the town and many married local girls and didn't want to return to Poland. Most of them couldn't go back anyway because Russia had taken over Poland and had put a price on their heads for fleeing their country.

Paul, our neighbour through the wall was such a man. He and his wife Helen had two small boys by now and they were trying to make a go of it too. Like mam, Paul started a garden and grew vegetables and tobacco. He used canopies off aircraft as cloches and the plants grew to an amazing size. I wonder to this day where he obtained the seed for the tobacco…

From 1947 the Polish Army sites had started to become vacant and by 1948 they were all occupied by homeless people. The number of people now living in and around Forres was growing steadily and the

,uncil had put up 50 prefabs between the railway line and Fleurs
,lace, so some families were rehoused. (*In order to meet the housing
shortage as World War II was coming to an end, Wilson Churchill announced
a Temporary Housing Programme in 1944. The program planned to build
500,000 prefab bungalows in Britain over the next four years. In fact just over
150,000 were built. They were expected to last for fifteen years but a few still
remain today.*)

By 1949 we had settled in for the long haul, all of us waiting to be
rehoused. 'Squatter' was still a dirty word and even the local dairy
wouldn't deliver milk to us. The milkman would only deliver the milk
to the bottom of the hill opposite Asher's shop. Being a large family,
we needed four pints a day and it was my job every morning before
school to go and collect it and I hated it. We had no bags or baskets so
I had to carry the four glass bottles in my arms all the way back up to
the hut. To my knowledge there were no deliveries of any kind made
to the people living in the huts except maybe mail.

Despite all this we children had great fun climbing trees, making
huts, paddling in the mill lade that ran from the pond right down the
side of the site to the Plasmon Oats Mill at the bottom of the hill, despite
being forbidden to go near it. During a long spell of wet weather it
could be quite a deep and fast flowing burn. The year before a toddler
had fallen in and drowned, which was dreadful but it never stopped
us.

For some reason there was an old mangle which had been left in the
middle of the site and we were always playing around there. My friend
and I decided to put, of all things, ping pong bats through the wringer
and I didn't take my hand away quick enough and my fingers went
through as well. It was a very heavy old mangle and my fingertips
were burst and bleeding. Naturally I couldn't write for quite a while
at school.

Expressly forbidden to go near this thing again, I still played with
it. Not long after my fingers healed, we were putting other things
through the wringer and you had to caw (*turn*) this huge circular iron
handle, which fell off the mangle and landed on my foot, crushing my

big toe and the two toes next to it. I remember seeing my toenails sticking up out of the bloody flesh. My friends had to carry me to my door screaming. Poor mam must have felt like screaming too. That was me off school for quite a while - again.

MUCH of this year was taken up by endless speculation by the grown-ups about when the new houses at Anderson Crescent would be ready. The Council had only been allowed to build a few to start with and there were over 300 families on the waiting list. There were hardly any workmen to build them and sometimes work stopped all together. As far as us kids were concerned, we'd found a new place to play in amongst the half-built houses. We had great fun but never a day went by without one of us getting skint knees and bruises all over. We were forever being chased away by workmen.

Things at school were still as bad as ever. Because of my 'accidents', I had a lot of catching up to do and as a result I always found myself in the lower half of the class. The system set up in school meant that the back row of the class was where the brainy kids sat and from there on everything went downhill. The teachers were still real tartars and the pointer and strap were always present and used quite freely. They put the fear of death into me. I couldn't wait for summer to come, just to get away from school and the town kids.

The Bogton Road Gang was still fighting with the Huts Gang and every so often there would be a raid planned and our gang would get wind of it. It seemed to me that they would both set off from their ground, meet up somewhere and have a great time swearing and ear bashing, then both gangs would retire to their own grounds bloodied but triumphant. There were never any real casualties on either side and I think both gangs enjoyed letting off steam. There were never any thugs or bullies to my knowledge, us girls were just a bit scared of them because they tended to posture about a bit *(show off)* when they knew you were looking at them. Some things never change do they?

Chapter 8
1950

In the December of 1949, my Granny Tough died. She had been ill for a long time and my Auntie Margaret had taken a year off school to nurse her but nothing could be done in the end. It was a very sad Christmas for all of us. It was decided that Auntie Margaret and Uncle John would come and live with us at the huts and Uncles Charlie and Wilson would go to live with Auntie Bess at Stoneyford. Granny's house had been a tied house and had to be given up after her death. Farm and forestry cottages were built for the workers and their families. If the worker died the rest of the family had to move out but Granny Tough was very lucky to be allowed to stay there until she died, rather than when Grandad Tough died earlier but when she passed the rest of the family had to move out.

Auntie Margaret had to go back to school for a few months to finish her education and then she got her first job at the Cluny Hill Hotel and continued to stay with us. During this time she was to meet the man she would eventually marry, Jimmy Donald. He used to come up to the huts to see her and they would go walking hand in hand. To me this was so romantic, being the age I was. Auntie Margaret still seemed more of a friend than an auntie to me, having lived within the Tough family for so long and I was happy for her, knowing how she missed granny.

Uncle Wilson was also very sad at losing his mother so soon after his father, who had died in 1946. He took her death badly and was so sunk in grief that he hardly spoke to anyone. The splitting up of the family affected him most of all. He wanted to come to us rather than stay with Auntie Bess but she insisted he should stay with her. It was an unhappy situation but he wouldn't be there long, as he would soon be called up for National Service.

We were now into 1950 and still no word of us getting a house. I hated the long walk to school, especially in the winter months. Anna, Joan, James and I all walked together. We became close friends in those years, simply because of our circumstances.

I was eight years old this year in April, my brother Jimmy was five and my sister Jean was three, all in the same month. I knew that if we didn't get a house soon that I would be taking Jimmy to school every day. I wasn't looking forward to that. Jimmy and his wee pal Robbie Chisholm were starting school the same day, so all the bigger kids would have to look out for them. The school was only a two minute walk from my Granny Fraser's house and sometimes mam would be visiting her in the afternoon and we would all walk home together.

Auntie Margaret left her job at Cluny Hill Hotel and went to work at the Ramnee Hotel. It was a live-in job so at least she would have a room to herself. Uncle John was still living with us. The first half of the year wasn't great for any of us. I was still unhappy at school, mam was unhappy with the housing folk and dad was the unhappiest of all because the Bobbin Mill had burned to the ground and all the workers were out of a job.

To cap it all, I had another one of my accidents. We always played jumping up onto the iron gates at the top end of the camp, which stopped people entering the Sanquhar Estate. At about waist high to an adult there was a row of six inch spikes with room enough between them for our feet to land. My right foot missed the footrest and my leg landed on a spike, right through my calf. My friend had to pull my leg off the spike and I remember to this day seeing a vein hanging out of the hole. My friends joined their hands together for me to sit on and they carried me home. That was more time off school for me. The wound was too big and open to stitch so I had to wait for it to heal from the inside and for new skin to grow over the hole. So far, I had not managed to have a full year at school, not that that was bothering me, I still hadn't taken to it.

In the summer of that year we were offered a house in Anderson

Crescent. It was one of the first to be ready and my Auntie Margaret, Hugh's wife and Uncle Hugh were also offered another one. We had to turn them both down because we couldn't afford the rent. Mr Liddell, the PE teacher at the Academy got the one we were offered. I was so disappointed I couldn't bear to pass the house. But mam and dad must have felt even worse.

The summer holidays came and went without anymore mishaps and I went back to school to start my fourth year. Jimmy started his first year. In October we had the best news yet, we were offered a house. I could hardly contain myself, I was so excited. It was 31 Roysvale Place and it had a lovely big garden. Mam and dad were so happy - at last we would have a proper home.

WE moved to our new home on 31st October, 1950, Halloween day. Uncle Tom did the flitting *(moving)* for us with his wood lorry. Although we couldn't go out guising *(trick-or-treating)* this night, mam had bought us wee bags of sweeties so we were quite happy to explore our new home and garden. It seemed so much bigger than our hut, with three bedrooms, kitchen, bathroom and living room. Most surprising of all was that we had electric lights throughout. The former tenants must have paid to have them installed. There were still gaslights on the walls though and there was also a gas cooker. There were open fires in the bedrooms as well as the living room. Our utility furniture, the only kind you could buy after the war, fitted in quite nicely. It was built to last and it served us well for years to come.

The next day I began my new life in the town. Anna and Joan called in for me to walk to school, as it was on their route. I was pleased to see them because I didn't know any of the kids on the new estate yet. I will always remember the first weekend of my life there. I was standing just inside our front garden gate, looking across at the houses opposite. Two children came out of two houses and came to their front gate and we stood and looked at each other. The boy was Gerald Gill and the girl was Violet Milne. The boy, who looked a couple of years older than me, said, "I'm Gerald and she's Violet, what's your name?"

I laughed and said, "My name's Violet too". The hand of friendship offered by Gerald that day has stayed in my memory all my life. He made it possible for me to integrate with new neighbours and children. Violet was to become a lifelong friend, along with Gladys, her sister, although she was two years older than us. Slowly I came to find my way around Roysvale and got to know the children who lived there. Down at the bottom of my garden and across the road in Castle Street were Mavis and Frieda Williamson. Mavis became a good friend throughout my childhood. Down the road a few yards lived Meggie Grant, another good friend. And up at the top of Castle Street, opposite where the ford is, was Ellen and 'Buzz' Sharp. Ellen didn't get as much freedom as we all did; her parents were quite strict. But in the years to come we were to become close friends. There was one other friend I made around this time, Jeannie Fraser. She lived at 2 Fleurs Place, just across the burn. She also became a good friend of mine into adulthood. And so the scene was set for the rest of my childhood.

Strangely enough, none of my new friends were in my class at school and only Mavis was to be in my class in the Academy. My good friends Anna and Joan were not in my class either. So I only played with my new friends after school. These new friendships didn't happen overnight. I was the new kid on the block and, because I was a squatter, their parents may not have liked them being friendly with me. I don't know, I have never known and maybe I don't need to, I realise now. Like all girls, we fell out and argued with each other. There was always name calling when we fell out, some of it quite vicious as we grew older.

The name calling was always the worst thing for me to bear, because inevitably it would get round to me being called a squatter and I had no comeback on that score except to walk away, trying to stop the tears from starting, because they always won in the end. But amazingly enough we all stayed friends into our late teens. Some things never change – I could see this happening with my own two daughters when they were young.

Chapter 9
1950-1951

By the winter of 1950 we had all settled in nicely in our new home. Auntie Margaret used to come home and spend the night with us on her day off. I used to love listening to her talk about what was happening at her work and about her boyfriend, Jimmy. She was always full of fun. All my uncles and aunts from mam's side used to visit once a week. It was great to have the house full, to see them smiling and laughing again. They had had a hard time getting over granny's death but they were getting on with their lives now. And of course they always brought sweeties for us kids. Now that we lived a bit closer to Granny Fraser, we often went round there for our tea on a Saturday night.

Dad visited Granny Fraser every Sunday and often Uncle Hugh went as well because, as I said previously, granny never left her house again. It was good for dad and Uncle Hugh to have a natter.

In the spring of 1951 both Uncle Wilson and Uncle Davy were called up to do their National Service for two years. We only saw them every so often when they came home on leave. Uncle Wilson wrote to me occasionally and I felt very grown up getting these letters. Of course I wrote back telling him all the news of the family.

This year Auntie Margaret, Hugh's wife and Uncle Hugh had their second daughter, my cousin Sandra. It was this year that they got a house in Fleurs Place. My friends Anna and Joan's family also got a house in Anderson Crescent. But there were still so many families living in the huts. House building was so slow that some of the kids lived half their childhood there. Many years later my friend Cathy and I talked about our time there and she told me that the reason she left home so young was because she couldn't stand the constant catcalls from the Forres kids. She went to America when she was 15.

IT was in late spring, as far as I can recall, that we had our first visit from Mr Smith, the Minister from Castlehill Church. He was to become a regular visitor. Jimmy and I were to attend Sunday school there. I was quite happy about that because it meant that I would be meeting new people. Jimmy was horrified. There was no way he was going to Sunday school. He was supposed to come with me and mam would get him dressed in his best clothes and we would set off. I was told to hold his hand all the way but half way there he would take off at the gallop and I could never find him. I had to carry on or I would be late and I hated to be the last one in. Jimmy knew he would be in for a tongue lashing from mam so he usually stayed away for ages and was always in a mess when he finally came home. Mam took to coming with us, holding onto Jimmy the whole way. She would see us into the side door to the hall, then go home again. But Jimmy was sly, he would come into the hall with me and mill around with the rest of the kids and when he thought mam was well down the road he would scarper. He was a good judge of time. The school was for an hour and I would find Jimmy loitering in Roysvale Park waiting for me and he would come home with me. This went on for a while and I didn't know how to tell mam. She found out for herself when she came to meet us one day and found Jimmy playing in the park. She told dad and he said there was no point trying to make him go when he was so set against it. So Jimmy won the day. But when Christmas came round he couldn't go to the party so, as we would say today, you win some, you lose some.

I WAS nine this year and I joined the Brownies, which I loved. I felt so proud of the uniform and the badges. Our meetings were held in Forres House. I attended regularly. Strangely enough I cannot recall any of my friends being Brownies. I stayed with them until I joined the Guides but I'm getting ahead of myself, that was a few years later. This summer

Guides & Brownies in Forres High Street
Courtesy of Raymond Miller

would be the first that I would have in my new home - I was longing for the summer holidays and was so looking forward to playing with my new friends.

We all remember the long hot summer days don't we and I'm no different. I remember waking up on a sunny morning and thinking of all the weeks ahead with no school, my idea of heaven.

But before that we had our Easter holidays and we were all looking forward to our Easter picnic and rolling our eggs. In those days there was a big field behind Roysvale, opposite where the Forres Academy is today and the ground sloped steeply up to the trees overlooking the loch. It was the perfect place for rolling our eggs. It was a great treat after a long cold winter. In years past mam and us kids would all go together but this year I was to take Jimmy and Jean, David being too young. We had great fun hard boiling our eggs, then painting them. Mam would make up sandwiches and we would have a bottle of National Health diluting orange juice to drink. We always hoped for good weather and only snow or rain would stop us from going. Then, we would have our picnic indoors, rolling our eggs on the floor.

That first summer was when I really got to know my new friends. We would all play every day. The estate was divided into four blocks of houses with a crossroad in the middle, which was very close to our house. We called this 'the squarie' and we all congregated there. At any time of the day or evening you would always find a few kids there. It was where our games started and ended. All summer long us girls would play 'skiffies', our name for hopscotch. We would play skipping, French and ordinary, playing in teams or pairs. We would sing made-up songs as we skipped. There was another game that was very popular, which had no name. We placed two house bricks side by side a few inches apart with a kindler across both bricks with the ends sticking out at each side. We would have another kindler in one hand and we had to hit one of the ends sticking out, making it fly up into the air. We had to keep it up by hitting it with our kindler, counting how many times we kept it in the air. Whoever reached the required number was the winner. In our own garden we always played hide and seek and the younger kids would join in. Mam used to grow rhubarb, the leaves were enormous and the little kids could hide under them. Every garden seemed to have rambler roses cascading over the fences and hanging onto the pavements and you could crawl in behind them and couldn't be seen. I used to think they should have called it Rosevale.

That year the Plasmon Oats Mill stopped making oats and started making cattle cake. The lorries would come in laden with grass and there would be mountains of grass in the parking lot. We kids had great fun jumping about on it and burrowing into it. We were never chased away. Some of the underneath grass was starting to ferment in the sun and we would go home stinking of it.

Plasmon Oats Mill
Courtesy of Raymond Mills

IN the early years when there were just us four kids, me, Jimmy, Jean and David, mam and dad would plan days out for us all. In the early summer we would all go to Balnagieth to pick rasps. David was still the baby so he would sit in the pram, with Jean sitting on the end as we all walked up the Grantown road, about two miles west of Forres. We were not alone, many young families did the same and it was a chance for mam and dad to have a gossip with other parents. We would have a picnic and lots to drink, as we would be out all day. Next day mam would make the jam. A wonderful aroma would fill the whole house and we would have our first tasting of it on our pieces.

Another great day out was a picnic down by river Findhorn on a Sunday. As usual, the two youngest were in the pram, dad would be laden down with food and us carrying towels. We would set off early. There would be no Sunday school that day. We always hoped to get a choice place on the riverbank because it seemed as if half of Forres had the same idea. The best place was beside the Bailey bridge; there was lovely golden sand for the little kids to play in and it was easy to keep a watchful eye on the older ones paddling. Dad used to swim in the deeper parts.

OPENING OF NEW BRIDGE

Hon. Mrs C. M. Murray, Moy House, cuts the tape at the opening ceremony at the new bridge over the Findhorn on Friday. Below—Mrs Murray, accompanied by three of the oldest residents of the district, make the first crossing of the bridge after the opening ceremony.

Forres, Elgin & Nairn Gazette 25 August 1948
Opening of the Bailey Bridge
Courtesy of Scottish Provincial Press

The ferryboat was still tied up on the opposite bank from the days before the Bailey bridge was built. Sometimes Mr Macintosh, the ferryman, would take us kids across the river and back as a huge treat. Then, when it was time for the picnic we would all be ravenous and the best treat of all was red and green lemonade. At last, no more National Health juice. At the end of the day we had the weary walk home. That road home seemed endless and we were so tired out from all the excitement and activity. But us kids soon recovered and would spend the long summer evening playing out in the squarie.

When the summer was particularly good, the best treat of all was to go to Findhorn on the green double decker bus. We had to queue to get onto it, because half of Forres had the same idea. It used to be jam-packed and if you didn't get on first time, you had to wait for it to come back for you. Like us, whole families would go down for the day, so we were laden with buckets and spades, towels, swimming gear, as well as the picnic. Both front and back bays were crowded with families, a sight not often seen nowadays, with everyone going abroad.

Findhorn is a lovely village five miles from Forres on the north-east coast. The residents have managed to keep it unspoilt and almost the same as it was 60 years ago. It is a wonderful bay for boats and yachts. Around the headland is a golden beach which stretches as far as the eye can see. The waters are safe for swimming on this beach but you have to be wary in the bay down by the point. The tide can be very fast and dangerous.

Directly across from the village and bay stretching the length of the bay is the Culbin Forest, which, when I was young, was known as the Culbin Sands. It is a huge area that used to have big sand dunes reaching almost to Nairn, about ten miles as the crow flies. It was a miniature desert and when gales blew from that direction they took the sand with it, which got into every nook and cranny in the village. It too had a beautiful beach and we often saw people being rowed across for a picnic or party. The salmon fishers who fished there with nets often obliged locals with a salmon or other fish and got a bottle of something for the favour. Of course there are no nets on the bay now.

At the end of the day out, we would all troop back to the village to wait for the bus by the stone piers at the harbour. The younger kids would be girnin *(moaning)* after a long day and mams and dads would be getting frazzled trying to keep us all together. If you couldn't get on the bus you had the long wait to contend with till it got back. But it always was a great day out.

Chapter 10
1952-1953

At the end of August it was back to school again. I would be in my fifth year and it wasn't getting any better. The only thing that interested me was books. I would read anything, mam's magazines, Jimmy's comics, my own girl magazines. I just couldn't get enough to read. The teacher took us to the library in Forres House and I thought I had arrived in book heaven. I couldn't believe the number of books I was allowed to read. From then on my nose was never out of a book and it has been that way all my life. So obviously I've got something to thank my teachers for.

During this school year I started to get to know my classmates and there were also boys my age who became good friends throughout our school years. Brian, Podgie, Eckie, Donald, Foxy, to name but a few. We were a mixed bunch and we all got on well with each other. Some of these boys were in the Boys Brigade and I would get invited to their parties at Christmas, along with other girls. I wanted new party clothes but I had to make do and mend, as mam used to say. I had a new kilt and cardigan, which I wore to all events. Money was still tight in our family, as it was in many others and we just had to go without and try to adapt.

The parties were held in the hall down Bank Lane. The boys had to come and collect us and see us home again. It was all so exciting. There would be the Sunday school party as well. Although we didn't have much money, we had the parties to look forward to.

WE were into the New Year of 1952 and I was back at school. The winters of long ago were always very cold with lots of snow and boys and girls of our age never wore long trousers. There were no tights for us girls like today and what all boys and girls wore were knee high socks. Our knees were always chapped and red. Our noses were always running with the cold and often we had to slog our way through lots of snow to get to school, even though we were in the town. The country roads were often blocked. We always made long slides in the playground and we would all queue to get a shot on them. We always had a long slide from the squarie almost down as far as where Roysvale Terrace is today.

There was one teenage boy who lived on the estate, who shall be nameless, who used to wait until one of us girls was on the slide and take a right run at it and try and knock us off. You really came down with a thump if he managed it. Our parents always gave that bit of road a wide berth in the winter because they knew we always used the same bit of road every year.

It was quite common for us to get snow in April, even into May sometimes. The winters were always long, cold affairs and we never seemed to be warm. There was no such thing as central heating in houses and the fires couldn't cope with the cold. We would be huddled around the fire and our backs would be freezing.

Going to bed was an ordeal. The windows would be frozen on the inside, making pretty patterns of ferns and flowers and your teeth would be chattering as you undressed as fast as you could to get into your ice cold bed with your hot water bottle. We had a mixture of stone and rubber ones. I always thought I'd need about six to defrost me. Getting up in the morning was a nightmare because the house was absolutely freezing, even though mam was always up early to get the fire going. We used to bank it up last thing at night but it always seemed to be out in the morning.

I always liked to see the buds coming onto the trees; it heralded the end of winter. As usual, we had our Easter picnic if the snow had gone. This April I would be 10, Jimmy would be seven, Jean would be five and would start school. David would be four years old.

At this time of year, if it was a dry spring, I would go with one of my friends to find pussy willows to take home to our mams. Usually we would find a tree up the burn or round the pond. The ground was usually covered with a carpet of wood anemones. Come May time the woods were a carpet of blue with the bluebells. And on the bank in front of Sanquhar House was a cloud of yellow with cowslips. It gave me a great feeling to walk through the woods by the burn and see all the wild flowers appearing once again. It was wonderful knowing that winter was finally over and we had all of summer to look forward to once again.

Violet (left) & friend Gladys as
Guides 1952

During this last school term I was beginning to like learning the three Rs and I rapidly started to move up the class. By the end of term I was in the second row from the back which was a great achievement for me. I was starting to feel good about myself. In the previous few years I had no self-confidence because of all the name calling and gaining that position in class gave me a great boost. For the first time I started to feel equal to everyone else.

IN February 1952 the King had died and Princess Elizabeth was declared Queen. Coronation day was the 2nd June 1953. We had a day off school and there were special parties for both schools organised. We were all looking forward to the celebrations. Mam bought me a new frock for the occasion. All children received a Coronation Day mug with the date of the Coronation and picture of the Queen's head engraved on it. It was a great day, with lots of jelly and ice cream, balloons and banners and flags flying.

n the same day, Everest was conquered by Edmund Hillary and erpa Tensing. It was a wonderful end to a great day. The following year Hillary and Tensing came to Forres and us school kids were taken to the picture house to see the film of them on Everest and to listen to their lecture. It was a wonderful and unforgettable day. Mountains climbed today are often televised and the climbers are well equipped against the conditions. It was a marvellous achievement for those two men way back then when all they had was basic equipment.

Picture House, Forres
Courtesy of Raymond Mills

The summer holidays came, with all those glorious weeks of freedom. We'd start the usual round of games in the squarie and I was allowed to paddle in the burn, which was only a few yards away from my house. When the weather was really hot I was allowed to learn to swim in the deeper pools. We would spend hours in the water by the ford catching bandies with our hands and a jam jar. The big ones we called kingies and queenies and the competition between us was all about catching the biggest ones. I always took mine home to show the rest of the kids and I would sit the jar under a bush that grew beside the back path. Jimmy did the same when he was allowed up the burn, so I didn't know if it was his or mine but one year mam was weeding the vegetable patch and she found a jar with the bandie in it and it had grown into a small trout. Its body was all twisted up inside the jar. She showed it to us when we came home from school and told us we had to remember to put the bandies back into the burn.

I was starting to explore further afield and some of us kids would walk down to Scotties Bridge. This is the bridge that crosses the burn at the West End of Orchard Road where the Brig Motel was. It was a semi-humpback bridge built with huge stones and a great parapet, about one and a half to two feet wide. We would often sit on it and watch the world go by or lean over on our chests and watch the fish dart about in the clear water.

This day, Morag Miller, dad's cousin who lived at the Burdshaugh huts as well and I were in the water paddling about to see what we could find. The burn had been up for a few days because of rain in the hills and now it was back to normal. We both spotted something glinting in the water and made a dash for it. I suddenly felt a stinging in my foot and looking down, there was blood colouring the water. I had cut my foot on broken glass. Suddenly I felt the pain and managed to make it to the bank. Blood was pouring out of my big toe and I was crying. Jimmy Mann the postie was passing and realized what had happened. He ran to the farmhouse and got a blanket, wrapped my foot in it and carried me over the bridge and across the road to Dr Adams surgery. Dr Adams refused to treat me because he wasn't my doctor, so Mr Mann had to carry me all the way home, blood pouring from my foot. Mam ran to the phone box and phoned Dr Bethune, who came and stitched me up. I thought my accidents were all behind me but it seemed not.

THOSE long ago summers were a sheer joy. We had weeks with no school and all the time in the world to play. Us kids who lived in that little corner of the town were very lucky to have the burn and the fields so close by. All of us could be found, if not in the squarie, up the burn

Veronica & Ian Shepherd Musik at the
Sanquhar huts 1952
Courtesy of Veronica Musik Tomlins

or at the ford. We were usually within shouting distance of mam although as Jimmy got older I was often sent out as dusk fell, calling for him up the burn. He was never a good timekeeper. Us kids knew the area like our own gardens and it was us who beat the paths, which are still followed to this day, although they are mostly used by adults nowadays. Every summer one of the boys in our group would climb up a big sturdy tree, just up from the ford and tie a rope swing to a thick branch which hung over the lower bather. A stout branch was tied onto the end to sit on. The swing would stay there all summer and we had great fun with it. It was safe enough as no little kids could get to it, either from the bank or the water and you needed a long branch to pull it to the bank to swing on.

Nearly every day around teatime this boy, who shall be nameless, used to come thundering up the path, kids scattering out of his way and whoever had the swing would let go to get out of the way. He would take a mighty jump off the bank and catch the swing as it swung out over the bather. Then he would hog the swing until he got fed up and would leave it hanging over the water out of our reach. He thought this was great fun but although us kids were fed up with him, we never said anything about it as he was a lot older than us. But maybe payback time would come and we would have the last laugh. One of my fondest memories of a summer morning is sitting on the back doorstep with a book, in the sun, or up on the coal bunker. I would sit there for hours if I'd nothing planned and any friends who called for me would join me on the bunker and we would plan the rest of our day.

Chapter 11
1953

Mr Smith, the Minister, had been a regular visitor. Every couple of months he could be seen of an evening cycling around his parish. He always visited the sick and anyone who needed comforting in any way. He asked me if I would like to join the junior church choir and I was happy to do so. Some of my friends and classmates who belonged to Castlehill Church were beginning to join. We had choir practice every Wednesday night and apart from the singing we all had a good time. There would have been about 24 of us and we could all sing and harmonize. Smithie was a very good teacher and was able to group us into soprano, alto, tenor and bass parts. As well as singing in church, we used to entertain the old folk in the Home opposite the church. We would sing there at Easter, Thanksgiving and Christmas. He would give us a party at Christmas in the Sunday school hall and in the summer he and his wife would organise cycle runs to Primrose Bay on the coast just along from the village of Hopeman and St John's Meads along the river Findhorn where we could have a swim. During the winter nights I'd get a wee slip of paper through the letterbox inviting me to silly games and a bite of supper at the Manse. It was Smithie himself who called these nights silly games nights. There were always about six of us plus Smithie and his wife. We always had dainty sandwiches and chocolate biscuits, which we all scoffed in double quick time. Of course every time I went to the Manse mam would always call after me to mind my manners; it was the Minister's hoose I was going to.

Smithie and organ player with the junior church choir, centre
Violet second row, far right. Joan Watson front row fifth from left

What we all thought was funny, as in ha ha, was that Smithie had a laugh like a braying donkey. Anything would set him off and we couldn't help laughing with him, not at him. No offence meant here, he was such a lovely man. I'm sure all who remember him will remember his laugh.

In the summer when he used to come a-calling in the evenings, we could see him cycling slowly up the road on his ancient bike. There would be a mad splatter through the house, everyone calling to each other, "The Minister's cummin, the Minister's cummin", and dad would make a break for the bedroom with mam calling after him, "Get back here Jimmy". Sometimes dad made it and mam had to make up excuses for him. But in the winter when it was dark, we got no warning, just the knock on the front door. We all knew it was the Minister because no one else ever came to that door and again there was a mad splatter to get the living room tidy. He always asked dad when he could expect him in church and dad always said never. Smithie always gave that braying laugh and I could hear the kids in the kitchen trying not to laugh. I was always trying hard to keep a straight face.

At this point in my life, dad was working up in Glen Affrick with other men from the area. He had gone there to work with Paul, our Polish friend, who lived on the other end of the hut with Helen, mam's friend.

THE North of Scotland Hydro Electric Board was building hydroelectric dams across the deep glens and dad was working on the Glenmoriston one. He would come home every Friday and go back every Monday. (*The workers were called the 'Hydro Boys'. The construction of such large-scale engineering projects brought a flood of workers to the Highlands, attracted by the relatively high wages - a skilled tunneller could earn up to £35 a week, ten times the wages of a local estate worker. The so-called 'Hydro Boys' were housed in large camps, where they lived for months or even years at a time. They represented a rainbow of different nationalities - not just British workers, but German ex-POWs, Poles and Czechs. And life was hard. They lived in camps of up to 3,000 men, away from home for months or years at a time, working in harsh and dangerous conditions Although no definitive accident statistics exist, it is known that many men lost their lives during that so-called Golden Age of hydro-electric construction. One camp of around 1,000 men is reported to have seen 22 deaths in a single year.*)

THE Council had been making progress with the building of Anderson Crescent and Paul and Helen had been given a house.

That summer I think mam was feeling a bit stressed and needed some 'me time'. She started to go to the pictures from 5.30pm till 8pm Mondays, Wednesdays and Fridays and I had to look after the kids, which was a bit of a bind. However, she gave me thruppence per night, which I could spend in any way I wanted. With ninepence a week pocket money I thought I was very well off. But I missed my friends, because they didn't always like to play in the garden.

Jimmy was a bit of a devil, as soon as mam had gone he would take off to places unknown and I couldn't stop him because I had to look after Jean and David. If he wasn't home by the time mam got home, I had to go and look for him. With dad working away in the week he took full advantage of this and knowing that he would get a clout on the lug and a right tonguing from mam didn't deter him. Mam's clout wasn't as hard as dad's.

I used to cram so much into those long summer days. If I wasn't up the burn I'd be climbing trees. Us girls were very much tomboys.

We would do anything the boys would do. At the top of Roysvale, where the school is today, the road was just a road with potholes and there was a fence alongside the field to keep the cows in. A row of trees ran along the fence and we had adopted a tree there. We all called it the easy tree. We played on another tree along by the ford too and we called this the hard tree. I would say to mam, "If anyone calls for me I'll be up the easy tree", etc. We would sit up in those trees for hours, talking 'girl talk'.

The field on which Forres Academy is built was pasture for Scottie's cows and sometimes there would be horses put to graze. The cattle and horses could cross the burn and graze on the other field, which belongs to the Academy today. Scottie was the same farmer who had the field up by the huts. His farm was situated on the bank of the burn where the flats by the health centre are today. When I was young the centre and surrounding houses area was a field. The farm backed on to the field.

Old Scottie used to walk up Castle Street to the field by the ford, take the cows down to the farm for milking every evening, then take them back again. He always carried a staff in his hand to guide them. When he got too old he used to wobble up on an ancient bike. Then his son took over and you could hear him cursing at the cattle up and down the road. This was a daily occurrence all through my childhood. Also a daily visitor was the milky as well as a horse and cart man and Mothers Pride the bakers van. Occasionally an 'Ingen Johnny' (*Onion Johnny*) would cycle around with his string of onions. (*Onion Johnny was the nickname given to Breton farmers who sold onions door to door in the UK. Although having declined in number since the 1950s the Onion Johnny was once very common. Dressed in striped shirt and beret, riding a bicycle hung with onions, the Onion Johnny became the stereotypical image of the Frenchman.*)

Best of all was the rag and bone man with his horse and cart and balloons on strings calling for rags and jeely jars. Mam always would find something to give him and we would get a balloon. That would be almost the only traffic on the roads. That's why we could always play on them in complete safety.

When I was about 10 or 11 years old I noticed posters stuck up around the town and, on reading them, I burst with excitement. I ran all the way home to tell mam there was a circus coming to town and it was to be in Roysvale Park. Jimmy and I couldn't contain ourselves. Having memorised the date of arrival, we decided to ask mam to wake us at 5am, so that we could go down to the field to see what was happening.

It was a lovely morning, the sun just up and we ran down the road to the hole in the fence and crawled into the park and lay down on our stomachs. It was a fantastic sight. Men were in the process of putting up the big tent and others were feeding the animals. There was a huge ring of caravans and animal cages and the animals were all making noises. It was a wonderful sight to us. Of course we couldn't afford to go to the circus but there was a menagerie and it didn't cost too much so we went to see the animals. Every day the circus was here, we would be down in the field watching the comings and goings

ANOTHER great happening in Roysvale Park was the arrival of the Gospel Tent, which was there for some weeks during the summer holidays. It was a big oblong tent, enough to take a large congregation. It was open to anyone who wanted to go in and we kids were always welcome. We would be given a drink of juice and some biscuits. We would sit on folding chairs facing a platform and someone would go up and pray. They taught us some hymns that we didn't know but they would hand out sheets with the words on them. The tunes were always catchy and soon we were all singing with gusto and clapping our hands to the music. We went most mornings and as a lot of us were choir members, we would start to harmonize. We were not shy about singing and we were made most welcome. People passing by would usually pop in and listen and often joined in themselves and of course this pleased the Gospel people. At night there were services held but I don't know if many people were converted. They continued to come every year in the summer all the years of my childhood.

ONE of the outings that were part and parcel of those years was the Saturday matinee in the picture house, which was the building where White's the removers firm is now. All the kids went to these and there would be great hilarity at some of the films. Us girls would say that we were Dale Evans and the boys would be Roy Rogers. The fun continued outside, chasing each other, laughing and having a thoroughly good time.

Half way through the sitting, the ice-cream girl would come down to the bottom of the cinema with her tray of goodies and she would shine a torch so that we could see them. Once or twice, if the picture house was full, the Manager or one of the ice-cream girls would walk down the aisles spraying disinfectant; it seemed to catch in your throat more than the smoke did.

One Sunday morning I was across at Mrs McDonald's to get her list for the Sunday papers and one of the sons was down at the bottom of the garden doing something and I could hear tiny squealing sounds. Being nosy, I went down to see what was going on. To my horror, there was a tin bucket full of water and there were about six new born kittens bobbing about mewing pitifully and every time they came up to the surface they would be poked down with a broom handle. I couldn't believe what I was seeing. I remember shouting at him to stop but he just laughed. I ran to get his mam but she said that they couldn't keep them and that it was quite normal. I ran across to my mam and told her and asked if we could have two at least but she said no as we had enough mouths to feed. By the time I ran back, there was no sound from the bucket. They were all dead. That was my first introduction to thoughtless cruelty to animals. Poor little things, dying within minutes of being born.

Over the years of our childhood, us kids would often find sacks weighted down in the burn, with kittens and puppies drowned in them. We played about in that water oblivious and just as well!

By the end of June the showies (*fairground*) came to town. Their traditional pitch was on the Mercat Green, the grassy area with the burn on one side and the other side where Dicksons Motors used to be.

What at a turnout they got every year. Whole families would go down, especially Saturday nights. Even my mam and dad would go and play tombola. One lot would come and go and another would follow. This would go on all through the summer and, towards the end of August, all the individual showies would end up in Nairn for the Nairn Games down on the links. Thursday and Friday were the build-up to the main event on the Saturday. Friday was a favourite night because everything was half price, fine and cheap for the kids. Saturday night it was full price. Everyone came away wearing *'kiss me quick'* hats. There were special buses put on from a bus stop by the Bank of Scotland and they ran day and night. There were always long queues coming and going. My parents never ever took us to the games. Seemingly, when I was four years old they took me to them and I had wandered off and they were in such a panic by the time they found me they swore they would never take any of us again. I had left school before I ever went again.

At the end of August we all went back to school. I was starting my second last year in the primary. That was three of us at school now, David was still the baby. This time, when school finished in the afternoon I had to go round to Granny Fraser's in St Ronans Road and do her shopping. I didn't have to go very far because there used to be two wee shops right next to the old Academy playground. One shop sold all kinds of things such as groceries, sweeties and lemonade. An old lady owned it and I used to be scared of her when I was younger. She hardly ever spoke and she always wore a long black dress and her hair was always pulled back in a bun. She looked like Queen Victoria. The other shop was 'Jockie Does' the baker. He was one of the best bakers in Forres along with Deas the bakers. I would then go along to the East End Post Office to collect granny's pension. Granny always saved thruppenny bits in a big old sweetie jar and I would get thruppence at the end of every week.

I was really starting to earn money. Old Mrs McDonald, who lived across the street from our side garden, to the right of Mavis's house on Castle Street, had called me across from my garden and asked if I would do her shopping for her every Saturday morning. She would pay me ninepence a week. So that was me sorted for years to come. It took nearly all morning to do her shopping because I had to queue at the Co-op butchers, then at the Co-op grocers. Every other week I had to make two trips because I had to renew the dried battery for her wireless *(radio)*. I had to collect this from Garrows wee shop down Tolbooth Street and the battery was heavy to carry. I also agreed to get Sunday papers from a grocery shop called Anderson's at Fleurs Place for her every week. Eventually the word got round about me getting the papers and I began to get them for six more people. That was very time consuming. There were always queues right out the shop door on a Sunday and by the time I had bought everyone's papers, including one for my parents, most of the morning had gone. But that was another one shilling and sixpence I had earned every week. The paper round was to be handed down to my brothers and sisters after I left school. That's continuity for you.

Chapter 12
1953-1954

Autumn came and brought with it the dark nights. We still played out in the squarie in the early evening. Sometimes we would talk about going plundering and occasionally we would go and get some apples from the apple grove. They were cookers and quite sour but we thought we were so brave trying to get them off the trees in the dark. The apples grew round the boundary of Applegrove School. It was a big angular grove with the farmhouse in the middle. I had never known these apples to be harvested, I didn't know why because there was always a bumper crop. It was such a waste.

At the bottom of Bank Lane there was an old house with a huge pear tree in the front garden. An old woman used to live there and if we knocked on the door and asked nicely, she would give us a bag of pears. She had no use for them and she used to say that we could come back every year to get some but she wanted us to knock on the door and ask first.

AUTUMN was the best time to forage for conkers. I was as eager as my brother to get some and dad used to take us to Dalvey Estate, where he used to go when he was a boy. We always had a great time looking for them amongst the dead leaves. That would usually be a Saturday if dad had to go back to Glenmoriston. Sometimes he would buy us a tuppenny bag of chips from Adam's chippy on the way home. That was such a treat.

This was also the time of year for hazelnuts. I would go up to Chapelton burn, just up from where the footbridge is now, with Jeannie or Meggie to gather them. There was a small grove of hazelnut trees there and we could climb up and get them and gather them off the ground. There were good crops every year. From there we would walk up the wooded slope into the sawmill that was there, and onto St Leonards Road, or cut through the sawmill and up onto Breakback, to pick some brambles.

Breakback is a steep hill overlooking the town and a lot of the boys from our area used it for sledging when there was a big snowfall. There used to be a 'right of way' from the bottom of the hill straight up, over and down the other side where anyone could walk. I am sad to say that houses are built there now.

Winter was upon us again, with all it entailed. Chapped knees, running noses, hot water bottles in bed, lovely ferns and flowers frosted on the inside windows. We really had freezing winters in those years. Nothing like today's winters, when sometimes we don't get any snow and hardly ever need to wear proper waterproof boots but fashion ones instead. In those days we would have given anything to have a pair of today's boots. All we had were welly boots and tackety boots for the boys (*leather boots with studs in the soles*). If you wanted gloves or scarves you knitted them yourself and probably used wool from an old jersey. Us girls learned to knit quite young. We were taught by our mothers. My mam wasn't a great knitter but she was always knitting baby clothes and she taught me stocking stitch so I could knit plain things like scarves.

Christmas was heading our way and we were making decorations and cards for our mams and dads. We all used to make miles of coloured chains for the classroom and we also made them for the home, we couldn't buy these things. With my saved up pennies I could buy mam and dad little presents. Things were still pretty hard going since the war but we all got an apple, orange, sweeties and a penny in our stockings. Jimmy and I always got a *Dandy* or *Beano* annual and sometimes *Oor Wullie* or *The Broons* and a board game and we always got presents from our aunties and uncles.

There were many parties to go to and we always had a good holiday. But all too soon the festivities were over and it was back to school for us.

It was always a long haul to the Easter holidays because in those days there were no mid-term breaks for us.

I was doing well at school at last. We were getting little tests leading up to the exams in June and I was doing so well that I was put into the back row in the class. The top of the class was always David Christie and Avril McDonald and I was now third. I shocked the teacher and myself.

Jimmy, Violet holding baby Raymond, David & Jean

IN March of that year, my brother Raymond was born. It was a surprise to everyone, my parents included. Mam thought she was done with all that. So did I. It now meant that I would be helping mam more, changing nappies, making bottles up and taking the baby for walks in the pram. Dad was still working up at Glenmoriston, so I was roped in to help in any way I could. I didn't like it one bit because I couldn't get out much to play. Raymond was born at home and mam's friend Helen, from the huts, came down to help with the birth. Many women had their babies at home in those days. You never had to leave the rest of your family to go into hospital and still had control of the home. All the women were well versed in childbirth and many times the doctor would come in at the last minute, or even just after the birth.

I, of course, was the runabout, running here, running there, up the street, down to the nurse's home at Invererne Road. It was a good job that I was fast on my feet.

After the lying in period after the birth and when mam was back on her feet, Smithie the Minister came down to see us and the new addition to the family. Of course he tried to persuade dad to go to church but he still had no luck. Raymond was christened at home.

By the summer holidays, mam started going back to the pictures (*cinema*) and I had to watch the kids again along with the baby this time. This taught me all I know about looking after a baby and I vowed to myself never to have any of my own.

THIS year my dad had a bad accident up at Glenmoriston. He was still working on the hydro dams when the accident happened. The crane operator didn't see dad and crushed him up against a wall. He suffered crushed ribs and punctured lungs. He was admitted to Raigmore hospital and was there for about six weeks. The afternoon it happened, the employers got in touch with Smithie the Minister and he came down on his bike to tell mam. She was very upset but Smithie was very good with her and us. He visited dad every week because he knew it would be hard for mam to get there a lot. He came down to the house often to see how we were doing and he did all he could to help us. When dad came home he wasn't able to go back to work right away. In the end he never did go back because mam didn't want him to. Times were hard for us but the rest of the family was there to help. He finally got a job with Briggs, which is Tarmac today. He was to stay with them until he died.

Briggs workers tarmacking Forres High Street
Courtesy of Raymond Mills

During these holidays I had a wonderful treat from Smithie. He came down to the house and asked my parents if I, along with two other girls, could go with him and his wife to the theatre in Aberdeen. I was over the moon. We were to see *Lace on her Petticoat*. It was a tale of female friendship and social difference on the west coast of late nineteenth century Scotland by the Scottish Playwright Aimee Stuart. I had to wear my 'Coronation' dress. It was the only good one I had and mam had bought new Clarks sandals for the occasion. It was so exciting. We had our own box in the theatre and I loved the play. It stayed in my mind for years to come.

At the end of August that year we all went back to school. I was in the last year of my primary education. It felt strange to think I'd be going across the road to the Academy the following year. This final year would be the decider on which class I would be going into when I went to the Academy. I continued to work hard and was keeping my place of third in the class. Being the big guys of the primary now, we really felt we were growing up and we lorded over the younger kids but not in a bad way. We just felt separate from them now.

Class Photo 1954 - Violet second row from bottom, sixth from left
Jane second row from bottom, second from right

It was to be a far busier school year than we'd ever had. We had more homework and more tests, getting us ready for the big test to come.

At the weekends we still went gathering nuts and picking brambles. Choir practice was every Wednesday night. We were still entertaining the old folk at harvest time and Christmas.

Christmas was not a holiday for many people in Scotland in those days and I remember walking up to the High Street to see dad when he was working on repairing pot holes in the road. The only day he got off was New Year's Day. I really felt sorry for him having to work when all of us were at home. It didn't feel right.

New Year came in as bleak as usual and 1954 was with us. The big push was on at school, getting us ready for the big exam in the summer term. Round about springtime we had a new addition to our class. I'll call this person Jane. She just appeared one day seemingly out of the blue. She was a petite little girl of our age and very shy. She was pretty, with thick mousy brown curly hair. It was a freezing day and all she had on was a short navy blue skirt and sandshoes, no socks and a small army blouson jacket. She never looked at us, just kept her eyes down as the teacher introduced us to her. She took the girl to a desk near the front. These desks were double and out of the blue she asked me to come and sit beside Jane and help her get familiar with what we were learning. Well, I was not happy about this turn of events. And over the next few days Jane never mixed with us in the playground, never spoke to other kids, she just stood in a corner till the bell went. I began to suspect that Jane was not like us and, after sitting beside her in close proximity to her, I realised that she was from a 'tink' (*gypsy*) family. I know nowadays how politically incorrect this is to call anyone that but in those days we knew no better. There were a lot of families of tinks camped down by the river on the Nairn road. It was traditionally a winter site for them. For the first time in a few years now, I felt the word 'squatter' reared its ugly head. I was the only one in the class from the huts and she was the only 'tink', so I felt that we were put together because of this.

I didn't voice what I was thinking but I was very angry. I did help Jane to integrate and when she started to come out of her shell, she was a very nice girl and very clever too. She was very dirty but I knew it was not her fault; it was the way they lived. Mam caught me scratching my head one day, so I had to let her inspect my hair. I knew what she would find and I hadn't wanted to tell her about Jane but she wrung it out of me and I got a right telling off. With all the other kids in the house I couldn't afford to have nits, they would spread like wildfire. I also didn't like the way she had to get rid of them. She used a steel nit comb and horrible smelling lotion and I knew I would have to let her do this but I hated it.

We broke up for the Easter holidays. It was time for exploring again with the winter behind us and, with the prospect of summer ahead, it was a good feeling. To shed our winter clothes at long last and dress in lighter clothes felt great. Out came the skipping ropes and bats and balls. All us kids had a new lease of life and we felt great, fit as fiddles and raring to go.

I decided to pay a visit to Anna and Joan up in Anderson Crescent and we went for a walk. I had not been round the crescent since the houses were finished. Everyone on our camp had been rehoused and I was happy for them. In the centre of the crescent, MacDonald Drive was built.

PEOPLE in our huts at Burdshaugh were the first to be rehoused but unbeknown to me, there were still people living at Mannachie and Thornhill. I went with Meggie one day to visit family friends and I didn't realise that we were going to the Thornhill huts. As we got to the top of the big hill over the railway on the Grantown road, I saw them down on our right. No one had been rehoused from these huts yet. I felt terrible as we walked into the camp, for some reason I didn't know people were still living here and I was shocked. Some mothers were sitting on their doorsteps with young children watching us. I wanted to turn and run. I felt very uncomfortable here and felt ashamed. I did not know why I felt this way but, with hindsight, I think I felt guilty because I had been out of the huts now for a few years and had forgotten about these people, still living in hope of eventually getting a house. These children were being called 'squatter' just like I had been. When I got home, I told mam where I'd been and she told me that my dad's cousin Weesh Fraser, his wife Rosie and their children were living on that camp. A few years later Ferry Road was built to rehouse them.

I WENT back to school after the holidays and the race was on to get us geared up for the Intelligence Test, which was to be called the Eleven Plus in later years. We were all nervous about this test, because it would place us in the various classes in the Academy. I was determined to do well, firstly for myself but also to show that having lived as a squatter doesn't determine the level of one's intelligence.

Week after week we were getting small exams to bring us up to the level for the test.

Meanwhile, I was still sitting beside Jane. She was doing very well in all the tests, racing ahead of many of the others.

Then the dreaded day came. I could see that I was not the only nervous one, we were all very quiet, not our usual selves. The teacher told us that the test consisted of one hundred and twenty questions to be answered in one hour. We were told to pick our pencils up, not to copy from anyone else and to put our pencils down when told. So, the race was on. I was very pleased with myself. I answered all the questions within the hour and sat back, glad that it was all over. My fate would be determined with the results and we wouldn't have long to wait. We would have them in a matter of weeks.

Meanwhile we were all told to think about our futures and what we wanted to do when we left school. I hadn't a clue what I wanted to do. All the adults that I knew were working in hotels or shops. I hadn't thought about my future and mam surprised me by saying I should think about taking commercial subjects in the Academy - shorthand, typing and bookkeeping. I just couldn't believe that my mam had thought so far ahead. I decided to go for that and when it was my turn to be 'interviewed' by the teacher, I said I wanted to study commercial subjects and hoped to be a shorthand typist. She said that was fine and that was that. The results came back in due course and we were all so nervous. To my absolute delight I had scored 119 points, David Christie had the same, so we were joint first in the class. I couldn't wait to get home and tell mam.

All the excitement had died down and we were back to more lessons as we headed for the summer holidays. A strange thing occurred one Monday when we were back after the weekend - we found a strange man in our classroom. He informed us that he was our new teacher till the end of term. We were all intrigued as to why the change. Also, Jane was absent for the first time. We never connected the two. It was weeks later when I was told that our teacher had taken Jane to the public baths in Forres House and had bathed her and washed her hair. Our teacher was dismissed and we never saw Jane again. She never attended the Academy. I have often wondered over the years what happened to Jane. She was such a nice girl and so intelligent. What a waste it was if she never got the opportunity to make something of her life. I'd like to think she outgrew her family's way of life.

Two weeks before we finished our last year in primary, I was told I would be in the 'B' class at the Academy. Mam wasn't happy about his because of the high mark I got in the final test and wondered why I would not be in the 'A' class. When I asked why, the teacher told me it was because I wanted to take commercial subjects. I didn't think any more about it until I noticed that girls from the 'A' class were taking these commercial subjects too. They told me that they were given the choice to take these classes. Again, I felt I was being treated like a second class citizen and it reminded me of the time I spent in the huts. For the last three years in the primary, I'd been getting prizes at the end of the school years, I came second in the Intelligence Test and pupils who came behind me in that exam, were put into an 'A' class.

I came to realise that there was a class system in our town and, if you didn't fit the criteria, you were not given the same opportunities to better yourself as others.

Chapter 13
1954

I started to grow up that summer. I still had my jobs at the weekend but I wasn't looking after my siblings so much because dad was working in and around Forres. I was really enjoying being free to come and go as I pleased. My friend Mavis was going to dancing classes in the British Legion hall, which I would have loved to attend but we couldn't afford it. Mavis decided she would teach me all the dances and we would go into the road outside our houses and dance for hours. I learned how to do the Highland fling, sword dance with crossed sticks and the sailor's hornpipe. We had a great time, dancing for weeks. In between we would be foraging up the burn, picking rasps (*raspberries*), digging for ground nuts and we were always chewing on mint from the Burnside and *sooky soorums* were growing everywhere. I found out years later that they were called sorrel. We seemed to have a built-in knowledge of what we could or couldn't eat or chew. If it was a good summer we would practically live in our bathing costumes, spending all day up the burn.

There was a big tree that grew at the edge of what we called the lower bather. This was a pool deep enough to swim in, just up from the fordie. As I mentioned before, one of the boys would climb up and tie a thick rope to a high branch and a thick stick was tied to the bottom of it so that we could sit on it and we had great fun swinging out over the pool. None of us ever fell in, we were very nimble. Even though it was a very wet summer, we still gathered to play but the rain did dampen our spirits.

After a week of rain the burn burst its banks and the river Findhorn broke out at the Red Craig, just up from the bridge where the Red Craig houses are today. It came straight across the field into the Pilmuir and came up as far as Councillors Walk, where it meets the ex-RAF quarters. The water came into the railway station and up Tytler Street and to the Victoria Hotel. It came out at Waterford and met the burn as it swept down from Sanquhar Loch, flooding fields and woods in its path. We could hear the roar of it from the house. There was word of the falls giving way, so mam packed loads of stuff in the old high pram and was all set to leave.

It was so exciting for us older kids, we kept watch on the burn and the falls but it was frightening to see the falls. The water was very close to the bridge and the spray was incredible. I quite understood why mam was scared - if the dam broke we would all be flooded in a matter of seconds.

When the floods started to subside, my brother Jimmy and his friend Robby Chisholm went down to Councillors Walk and found a huge salmon trapped in a pool. It was at least 10-12 pounds in weight and they carried it home to Roysvale between them. We were all amazed.

Meanwhile the boys had been busy tying a rope swing to a huge tree on the bank where the sheltered housing flats are built today. In those days that bank of the burn was covered with trees and bushes. The footbridge was still up at the ford. Also the mill lade coming down from Sanquhar pond emptied into the burn there, so there was still a raging torrent there.

Of course I had to have a go on the swing. I was terrified but if the boys could do it so could I. I only went on it once because it was so scary but no-one fell in. Mam would have had a heart attack if she knew what I was up to. But I felt I had to prove to the boys that I could do anything they could.

DURING my teenage years, my good friend Cathy and I used to picnic by the river. Cathy lived on the Moy side of the Bailey Bridge. (*The Bailey bridge was a type of portable, prefabricated, truss bridge. It was developed by the British during World War II for military use and saw extensive use by both British and the American military engineering units.*) Her father had been the ferryman before the bridge was built. The ferry used to cross from the Forres side of the river to the Dyke side before the Bailey bridge was built. The family lived in a cottage quite high up on the river, in the hamlet of Moy and told me that they had all been evacuated to the Town Hall during the flood and, when they were allowed back to their homes, everything had been destroyed. The water had been up to the ceiling in the houses and had left a foot of mud behind when it had receded. This had happened more than once to her family.

There was so much destruction done by the flooding. At the lower end by Waterford, all the farm fields were inundated with water and with the river and burn joining up, it flooded the whole of the low lying farms. It joined up with Findhorn Bay and it was all just a sea of water. There were no trains or buses running from Nairn or Inverness and we were cut off on that side of Forres.

At the ford at Burdshaugh, just up the road from my hut, the water was lapping at the road edge on our side and had flooded out into the old Plasmon Oats Mill. So even if we were to use the footbridge we would be into flood water on the other side. My friend Jeannie and I couldn't get together unless one of us walked all the way round by Scotties Bridge and back up to Fleurs Place, or vice versa.

This all happened in August and before I was to go back to school, I had another great treat. Smithie came down on one of his usual visits to my family and asked my parents if I would be allowed to go down to Edinburgh for the day with him and his wife. I think it was Anna and Meggie that were to go as well. I couldn't sleep that night for excitement. My uncles all gave me some money to spend, which was really good of them, they probably knew mam couldn't give me much. We started out at the crack of dawn in his lovely grey roadster. The weather was fine and we had the hood down. We all sang songs from our choir repertoire and had a great drive down. We went to the Zoo, climbed the Scotts Monument and went for a walk through the Botanical Gardens. At the end of the afternoon we all went to Woolworth's to spend our pennies. We drove back home in the night hours, all of us kids dozing in the back. It was a wonderful day out and we were all very grateful to our Smithie.

Forres Academy Primary Department 1939
Courtesy of D R Forester

Chapter 14
1954-1955

I was entering a new period in my life now. Going on to the Academy was a daunting thought. We were now going to be small fish in a big pond. Our school uniforms consisted of a grey skirt and green blazer, white shirt and a purple, yellow and green tie. My Auntie Bess had bought me my school blazer and she gave it to me on the Sunday before school started on the Monday. I was so pleased with it I put it on and ran across to show Mavis. She had just got a set of stilts, which I'd never seen before and she gave me a shot of them. I hopped onto the stilts with my blazer still on, wobbled about on them for a few steps, then my foot slipped off one, the stilt caught under my armpit and tore the arm of my new blazer almost off. I couldn't believe what I'd done; I was scared to go home because Auntie Bess was still over at mam's. But I just had to take the bit between my teeth and brave the storm. And what a storm it was. I've never had such a tongue lashing and I knew I deserved it. Mam knew someone with an old sewing machine and had the blazer mended in time for school on the Monday morning. I felt really bad about it, especially because Auntie Bess had been so kind to me. All my family knew that going onto the Academy was important to me.

Monday morning started with assembly for prayers, then on to find our first classroom and meet our home teacher for the year and be given our timetable for all classes. Our class was made up of kids from all outlying villages including Findhorn and Kinloss. There were a lot of children from those villages because of the RAF camp, so we had a great mixture of kids. There were a few kids from my old class in the primary, so it was a case of us getting to know the strangers but we all mixed well.

ANOTHER event was to happen in our family in October. My second sister Fiona was born. Over the past months I tried to deny what my eyes were seeing, because I was fed up of having babies in the family. I felt like I had become a part-time mother. Some of my friends had been jeering and laughing at me about mam having so many children. I felt embarrassed about it all. To make it worse, mam kept me off school to look after the rest of the family. Mam's friend Helen was there for the birth as usual and she called me through to see the baby after the birth but I wasn't interested. I heard mam say to Helen, "What's wrong with Violet?" and Helen replied that I was a bit jealous of the baby, which wasn't the case at all. I simply was not interested. I knew that I would end up looking after another baby with never-ending nappies to change and bottles to make up. Again I swore to myself that I would never have children.

Once mam was on her feet again, Smithie the Minister came calling to see the baby and see how mam was. We got no warning as usual and dad was 'ben the hoose' *(in one of the bedrooms)* so didn't hear the knock at the front door and the kids were playing in their bedrooms. The first he knew about it was when he walked into the living room and saw Smithie sitting in his chair by the fire. His face was a picture to behold and I had to look away or burst out laughing. Every time the Minister came to our house, he tried to persuade my father to go to the church. Dad always refused to go and would avoid Smithie at all costs. Smithie was his usual jovial self and congratulated dad on the new baby. My brother Jimmy had been in the kitchen when he heard Smithie's voice and tried to make a dash for it out the back door. However, mam caught him and dragged him into the living room telling him in a whisper to behave himself and sit down until the Minister went. The usual cup of tea was made and biscuits were offered, with mam giving Jimmy a murderous look as he tried to grab one and then Smithie got down to business.

Once again there was a battle of wills between dad and Smithie about the christening of Fiona. Dad saying he wanted it done in the house as usual, Smithie trying to persuade him to come to the church.

With this discussion ongoing for years, it seemed a kind of dance, with dad ducking and diving and the Minister waltzing rings around him. I could be a prompter here if they forgot their words. But out of the blue, my dad gave in. Fiona was to be christened in Castlehill Church. Mam was over the moon and thanked Smithie for his success with dad.

Fiona (left) with friend right, Alan below

When Fiona was six weeks old we all went to church as a family, to see her christened. Of course we had to be dressed up and that was a problem - there were just too many of us. It was decided that us kids would get one new item of clothing and the rest had to have hand me downs. Mam was dressed quite nicely, dad still had his demob suit but he had to get a new dress shirt and tie, which he complained about constantly. But the worst thing for him was he had to get new teeth. Most of his teeth were missing but it never bothered him. So when mam told him that a trip to the dentist had been organized, he nearly choked on the tea he was drinking. I don't know if he was scared of dentists but I had never known him go to one. We were all so used to seeing him with two thirds of his teeth missing, that we couldn't imagine him any other way. We loved him, teeth or no teeth.

Even so, he duly got his new set of teeth but he couldn't speak with them in. He told mam that he wasn't going to wear them, no-one would know, he'd keep his mouth shut in church. He tried every which way not to wear his teeth and mam practically had to shove them into his mouth on the day. We all set off, dressed in our finery, dad with his teeth in, Jimmy sulking because he had to go to church, hanging back, dragging at his tie, knowing that dad wouldn't tell him off because that meant he had to speak!

Mam told me later that he couldn't get out of the church quick enough. As soon as he was outside, he took his teeth out and put them in his pocket. He said that he was not putting them in his mouth again, even though there was to be a christening party back at the house and the Minister was coming by for a sherry, to wet the baby's head. Dad hated those teeth and only wore them again for weddings and funerals.

FIONA was different from us because she was so spoilt when she was a little girl. She had been born with a red birth mark across her forehead which trailed down to the top of her nose. It was a bright mark and it faded over the years but when she threw a tantrum it would come up on her face. Because none of us had any blemishes it seemed to scare mam and dad so she got away with everything. If she didn't get her own way she would throw herself onto the floor and kick and scream until she did. This caused the birth mark to appear. Such a fuss was made of her when this happened and us kids would be left gritting our teeth. We were never to chastise her, never smack her if she was bad, with the result that she got away with murder. She would hold her breath until she was going blue and mam and dad would be going frantic. This worked for her for many years, she even tried it in school but they were having none of it. They had seen it all before. It may have continued for longer but her place as baby of the family was to be usurped by the birth of the youngest of the family, my brother Alan. Fiona was about three when he was born.

WHEN the Tattie Holidays came that year, I found another way of making money. Our sewing teacher wanted someone to pick brambles *(blackberries)* for her. She was going to send them south and she would take as many as we could pick. She said she would pay sixpence a pound and supplied us with baskets, which held 10 pounds in weight. This was right up my street because I loved picking berries. I did a deal with my brother Jimmy and agreed that we would split the money evenly. Every weekend we went out at the crack of dawn, picking berries all up the burn and around Sanquhar and we would usually pick a full basket every weekend. That gave us five shillings between us. We made a tidy bit of money over the autumn and we could spend it however we wanted to. Mostly we bought annuals, books and comics to read or go to the first house of the pictures at the weekend.

This berry picking continued over the three years that I was at school. During the summer holidays children from the Academy could go raspberry picking to Blairgourie in Perthshire for a few weeks. That was where most of the rasps in the shops came from in those days. My friend Meggie went every year. I pleaded to go but was never allowed. Meggie used to come home with lots of tales to tell, she said it was great fun and you got paid for it.

The only way for us kids to get any money in those days was to run errands like I was doing, or pick berries as the seasons turned. Most boys would get a message boy's job or do a paper round. Message boys would take deliveries from the butchers, bakers, co-op and other shops and deliver the goods to customers around the town. Every shop had a delivery service in those days and they all needed message boys. They used to ride on a great big heavy pushbike with a huge iron basket in the front, which held the grocery bags and other goods.

Sometimes the boys would give us a hurl *(lift)* in the basket for fun. I remember when I got a wee hurl, the boy lost control of the bike and it went straight into the holly hedge. I was stabbed from top to bottom!

Country boys would do jobs on farms. We could all find wee jobs if we wanted to and we were encouraged by our parents to do so, as we would all have to work for our living when we left school.

Once I had settled into the new life of the Academy, I began to enjoy it. Mavis was in my class and we did lot of things together. Meggie was in the next year as she was a year older than us. Jeannie, Violet and Ellen were all in our year. Gladys, Violet's older sister was two years ahead of us. We were a loose-knit group of friends, all coming and going together.

I particularly liked learning dances. We had a Christmas dance every year and leading up to Christmas we learned lots of new dances. I joined the choir and we competed with other schools. I enjoyed PE and I was learning to sew, cook and bake and enjoyed these subjects as well as the 3Rs.

For the 11 o'clock playtime break, we were allowed to go outside the front gates to go to Jockie Doe's shop for a pinkie, which was a bun covered in pink icing, a firm favourite with the kids, or a butterie which was a saltier, flatter and greasier croissant, named after their high lard content.

Soon after I started the Academy the school put a stop to that and Jockie Doe used to come round the school railings with a huge basket and sell his wares through the bars. In those days we still got half a pint of milk each from the school if we wanted it. We were only allowed to go out onto the road if we had to cross over to get to the new classrooms, which had been built inside the primary school playground. The population of Forres and environs was growing.

Christmas came, with the usual round of parties, the school party, the Boy Scouts party and the choir party. It was great to have all those to go to; it broke up the holidays nicely. The winters were so long in those days and always cold. Sometimes the school buses couldn't make it to collect the country kids because of the snow-blocked roads. Trains would get stranded, buses too. You just didn't know what each morning would reveal. But us town kids always had to slog it through the snow. We had to watch out for snowballs and we had great fun slipping on the slides we made in the playground. We hoped our shoes or wellies wouldn't let in slush and make our feet wet. Us girls still had bare knees because we didn't have long trousers in those days. The boys, of course, wore long trousers now that they were in the Academy but we took it all in our stride because it was our way of life, there was no other.

The winter months slowly passed and spring was always a long time coming but finally we would be into April and Easter would be with us. I was 13 in April, Jimmy was 10 and Jean was eight years old. I was finally a teenager and had my first birthday party. I was amazed that mam let me have one and she managed to keep the rest of the kids out for the afternoon. All my friends came and we had a great time and my uncles and aunts gave me little gifts.

Over the past few years, Uncles John, Charlie and Wilson had all married and were getting on with their lives. Auntie Margaret had married Jimmy Donald, her childhood sweetheart and was living with us. Jimmy played the accordion and was trying to start a band. He was always practicing with his brother Freddy. I loved music of all sorts and he got me a small accordion and I taught myself to play it during the long winter nights. It was a grand hobby. Mam and dad must have suffered in silence, what with me in one room and Jimmy and Freddy in another, playing different tunes.

Fiona & Alan with friends

Chapter 15
1955

We had reached the summer term and my first year in the Academy was nearly over. We were to put on a concert in the town hall this term. The choir had been practicing for quite a while and we were going to sing the songs that we sang in the yearly competition in Elgin. Everyone was excited about the concert because it didn't happen every year.

In our sewing class we made costumes out of crepe paper, which were sewn onto any old dress we had at home. The dress wouldn't be seen, as the paper would cover it. It was great fun making these costumes. In the gym, we were practicing an underwater dance to the music of Swan Lake. We were supposed to be sea anemones waving about under the water, all dressed up in our pinks, yellows and greens. It was very effective - we had all done well with our dresses and you would never guess what we were wearing under all that crepe paper.

On the last day of our sewing class we were all rushing to finish off our costumes. I was sewing with a pin in my mouth and someone said something that made me laugh and I swallowed the pin. I told the teacher and mild panic ensued. The teacher had to tell Mr Skinner, the headmaster and he had to phone a doctor, who said that I was to go home right away and wait for the ambulance to come and take me through to Raigmore Hospital in Inverness.

I was devastated. I didn't want to go because I would miss the concert after all that sewing and practicing. I was in tears but I had to go and I got home the day after the concert. I was so mad with myself, having missed everything. Up on the wall of the sewing room was a notice, *'No pins or needles in mouths'* for all the rest of the years to come.

DURING this time, mam was working a few hours in The Carlton Hotel. Mrs Ewing, the owner, knew mam from her time there before she got married and had asked if she would like to work an evening or the weekend when dad was at home. Now that I was 13, she asked mam if I would like a small job too. It would be at the weekends making toast/breakfasts and washing dishes in the pantry at the back of the dining room. I was pleased to do a grown up job and I could still fit in my other wee jobs and have most of the day to myself. Although I didn't get much money, I had to give most of it to mam to help with the housekeeping. I learned very early in life that you had to work for a living and pay your way.

Outwith my wee jobs I still had lots of time for fun. I started to explore further afield into the countryside, often with Jeannie or Meggie. We would take a walk up to Lime Kilns to pick wild daffies *(daffodils)* in the spring or up to Blairs Loch in August to gather blaeberries for jam, or just to eat. On our explorations, if we got hungry, we would get a neep *(turnip)* out of a field, hack it against a barbed wire fence to get some of the skin off and do the rest with our teeth. We were never really hungry with all the berries and nuts around us.

A new friend I made that year was Hilary, who came to stay for the summer with relatives on the squarie. Mavis, Hilary and I spent the best part of that summer together.

At the back end of Sanquhar Loch were three islands, a big one, a medium one and a small one. We had found a way onto the big one. At the bottom of the steep bank bordering one side of the loch, we had discovered a hidden, overgrown path-cum-bridge just level with and sometimes under the surface of the water. It was all boggy around and about it and it was our secret. The three of us would set off mid-morning with a lemonade bottle of water and a piece *(jam sandwich)* and we would spend all day on our island.

This island seemed to enchant us and we were always desperate to get back to it. When we crossed the path and walked onto the island, it became a different world. The ground was covered with mulch and dead leaves, very soft to the foot but completely dry. The trees grew there in profusion and ran along the ground before reaching for the sky. It reminded us of palm trees we had seen in the pictures and we could run up them like monkeys and swing about on the topmost branches. We'd sit for hours high above the loch, swaying in the breeze. We would have a tree each, our favourites and sing at the top of our voices. We all loved music and the most popular songs were from *Oklahoma* and *South Pacific*. The romantic ones were our favourites – at our age romance was so mysterious and exciting and we would swoon over the male singers of that era.

We decided we would build huts for ourselves and see who could make the best one. Sad to say, we broke branches off evergreens to make them without a thought. We saw no harm in doing this in those days.

This took up most of our summer holidays that year and no one, to our knowledge, came onto that island. Our half-built huts were never disturbed. We used to whistle if we saw other kids walking along the loch path and we would see them looking all around to see where the whistles were coming from but they never saw us, high up amongst the branches. Even when it rained we were kept cosy and dry with the canopy of leaves above us. That was a perfect summer for all of us. I like to think Hilary went home with happy memories of our summer on the island.

Many years later I took my young daughters to the island. I could still find the secret path. They loved it and climbed the same trees that I did so long ago. Just a few years ago my daughter Joanne told me that her daughter was spending days in the summer holidays with her friends building a hut on the islands on the loch. It gave me such a strange feeling of history repeating itself. I was so glad to know that kids today still found pleasure in doing those simple things and that some of them still knew how to enjoy being children.

TOWARDS the end of those holidays, I had a lovely surprise. Smithie had been down to visit mam and dad and to ask them if they would allow me to go on a three-day trip with some others in the choir, including my good friends Anna and Joan. I was over the moon. He was such a good man, our Smithie, he took us to see things that we could never afford to do. In those days no-one had money to spend on frivolous things like trips.

We were to go up the east coast to John-O-Groats, along the top of Scotland and down the west coast. There were four of us kids and Smithie and we set off in style in his huge grey roadster with the top down. When we started we were in high spirits. Joan had not been well for a long time, so it was a treat for her. She only managed to make it to Brodie, she was so sick. Smithie put her on the first train back to Forres. We all felt bad for her.

The furthest I had been north was Inverness and that was to the hospital, so I was really excited. We travelled up the coast above Inverness on a single track road, on the edge of towering cliffs and we all took a turn sitting in the front seat. I was amazed how desolate the country was the further away we got from Inverness. It was mile upon mile of desolation. It had a rugged beauty to it but it brought home to me what the Highland Clearances meant. (*About 250 years ago, after the Battle of Culloden, which the English won, any clans who had taken part in the battle were made homeless. They were often forced to watch their homes burnt to the ground by the English soldiers. Even those who didn't take part in the Battle were forced from their crofts because their lands were given over to English Lords who forced the people out. They wanted the moors for their grouse shooting and the rivers for fishing. There was no other livelihood for the poor Scots. They left in droves for Canada and Australia, hoping to find a better life for their families as indentured servants. (Indentured servitude refers to the historical practice of contracting to work for a fixed period of time, typically three to seven years, in exchange for transportation, food, clothing, lodging and other necessities during the term of the contract. They were not paid cash and most became helpers on farms or house servants.) This dark history of Scotland came to be known as the* **Highland Clearances.***)*

There were derelict tiny cottages, some only a pile of stones to mark the place where families had lived and died. Smithie told us about it as we drove along and I felt so sad, thinking that children like us would have had to leave all they knew to cross the ocean to a strange land, not knowing what was ahead of them. It may have been exciting but also terrifying.

We arrived at John O' Groats in the late afternoon and Smithie had another great treat for us. We were to spend the night in the Duncansby Head Lighthouse with the lighthouse keeper and his wife. Once we had met the couple and put our bags in our rooms, there was plenty of daylight left for us to hike up to the top of the cliffs to see the Stacks standing just off the shore. They are a strange and impressive rock formation, which rise out of the sea above a narrow shore platform. The Great Stack is over 60 metres high and rises above the summit of the adjacent cliff. They were rugged and breathtaking. The wind was strong and the sea was wild against the Stacks. The Stacks are rumoured to resemble Mordor, a fictional site out of the popular book *'Lord of the Rings'* by J R Tolkien. As we came down the cliffs we had our first good look at the lighthouse. Of course it was round and all the rooms were round, with a spiral staircase going up to the top. The living quarters were on the ground floor. It was deceivingly roomy. They had an open plan living room/dining room/kitchen, with a big solid wood table in the middle. It was all set for teatime and seven of us sat very comfortably round it. After we had eaten, the lighthouse keeper asked us if we would like to explore the lighthouse with him and we were overawed with it all. We went right up to the top, where the light shone out over the water. We could walk right round the top and look out to sea. What amazed us was the light itself. It was a tiny mantle in the middle of reflectors which the keeper lit every evening and this shone a light out over the sea for miles, as it slowly turned back and fore.

We went to bed early that evening, as we were very tired. It had been a long, exciting day. We had seen so much and it was a lot to take in but we were up bright and early next morning ready for our next adventure. We ate a hearty breakfast, thanked the lighthouse keeper and his wife and then went down to the tiny post office on the cliff head to buy postcards to keep, which would remind us of our stay in the future.

We continued on our journey and followed the single-track road, which ran by the edge of the shore for miles. The beaches were golden and isolated, with only the sea birds swooping and diving. The countryside on our left was desolate, with hardly a building in sight. The sun was up and it sparkled off the sea, almost blinding you if you looked too long at the water. We turned inland before Cape Wrath and made our way down the west coast. I had never seen such scenery except in books; it was truly beautiful and so rugged. We saw little coves and bays and, as the road snaked up and down amongst the cliffs and valleys, wild flowers were growing in profusion everywhere you looked.

The lighthouse keeper's wife had made us a picnic and we stopped to eat overlooking a lovely little loch.

Luckily we were not bothered by midges (*small, two-winged flying insects similar to gnats. Biting midges fly in swarms that follow you around and are famously vicious*). My father had warned me how bad they were on the west coast but we were having a charmed little holiday and no-one was bitten.

We started off again and Smithie told us we were heading for Lochinver, where we were to stay the night. This was a tiny village on the side of the loch with mountains and valleys around us. Our hotel was overlooking the loch and our room had a wonderful view. We were all quite tired as it had been a long day. Smithie suggested we all have an early night. Nobody argued with that and I fell fast asleep as soon as my head touched the pillow. I was awakened later by music. I got out of bed to look out of the window and was amazed to see a lone piper out on a jetty playing his pipes. He was silhouetted against the loch but I could see he was dressed in a kilt. It was a scene that was to stay with me all my life. I told everyone about it in the morning but no one else had heard it.

Next morning, after a hearty breakfast, we set off for Inverness and then back home. It was a lovely little holiday and I'll always be grateful to Smithie for showing me such a lovely part of our country and for the history lesson about The Clearances, sad though it was. I think he wanted us to know and to remember what had happened to our countrymen and women so long ago.

I MENTIONED earlier that my friend Joan, Anna's sister, did not keep in good health. She was in and out of school for a long time. When she had to stay at home her lessons were sent up to her in Anderson Crescent. She finally was too ill to even attend school again though she still did her lessons. Between the ages of 15 and 16 she died of leukemia. She was made a Dux of Forres Academy of that year. We were all so saddened, she had fought so hard but it wasn't to be.

Sanquhar Loch 2012
Courtesy of Peter Jones

Chapter 16
1955-1956

I discovered that I had something that the other kids hadn't – a pair of roller skates. I loved them and would go out on them as often as possible. My Auntie Connie in Canada had sent them over to my Uncle Davy after the war in the early fifties. He had grown out of them and when granny found them in the glory hole *(under the stairs)*, Davy told her to give them to me. Everyone wanted a shot of them. The roads around Roysvale were perfect for roller skating, they were so smooth with no ruts or holes. I would spend hours just skating around. Another thing that Auntie Connie would send over was comics, which were nothing like our comics. My friends and I were reading about *The Simpson's* decades before the show came on telly.

I told you earlier about our swing over the lower bather on the burn. Well, we made one every year, one of the boys would climb the tree and tie the rope in a knot to the usual branch and it would remain there all summer. This year had been no different and we were always to be found at the swing in the evenings. But we were still being bothered by the boy who shall be nameless. This particular evening, Frankie Lewis, a cousin of Jimmy Laurence, whose garden bordered ours, was up on holiday for the summer and we had told him about this boy. Frankie said he would climb up the tree and when the boy was coming, he would quickly undo the knot but still have the swing attached to the branch.

Well, it all went swimmingly. We heard the boy's tackity boots thundering up the path and we signalled to Frankie. The boy came and, brushing us all aside, took a leap off the bank for the rope. Frankie and the boy both fell together with a tremendous splash into the bather.

How we laughed. The air was blue with curses, as we all scattered to the four winds. It worked, he never came again.

The summer holidays came to an end and I went back to school for the second year in the Academy. With one year under my belt I felt quite confident now. My friend Joan Watson had not been well this year and had missed a lot of school but she was getting homework to keep her up to speed with the rest of us. The next set of holidays would be the tattie holidays in October. They were called that because pupils were allowed three weeks off school to help the farmers get their crops of potatoes harvested. You had to apply to the headmaster to have these weeks off and you had to pick tatties. I thought this would be quite good fun and told mam about it. So I applied, was accepted and was told where to go to be picked up on the first day.

Picking the tatties was back-breaking. We were given a stent *(a particular length of ground to pick)*. The tractor would go in between the drills and unearth the tatties and we had to pick all of these tatties and put them into baskets. The tractor always came round too quickly for the next stent. I've never felt so sore in my life. I ached in every muscle and bitterly regretted applying for it. Those three weeks were never ending. Some of the boys were just bullies and chased us girls all over the fields. We got our mid-day meal from the farmer and it was always a hearty meal. They must have known we would be starving. At break times we always got tea, scones and pancakes baked by the farmer's wife.

I think worse than the picking was the harrowing. Once the field was picked, the farmer brought the harrower in and attached it to the tractor, which then proceeded up and down the field, dragging the harrower, which looked like a giant rake, uncovering any potatoes we missed. We had to walk in a line behind the machine, picking up the tatties raked up. It was back-breaking at the end of a full day's picking. I can honestly say those weeks were the longest I've known and I was glad to get back to school.

I was allowed to buy a pair of 'flatees', which were the shoes in fashion, or slip-ons as they were called. I felt very grown up with them on my feet, no matter that they pinched like heck. Talking about slip-ons, Meggie and I went for a walk up round the loch one afternoon in the autumn. Meggie had on her new shoes her mam had just bought her. We went up the far side of the lake, round to Chapelton burn and walked up towards the farm. As we looked down the bank we could see a tree, which had been blown down over the burn, landing well onto the other side. As we had walked some way up the burn, we decided to cross over it using the tree as our bridge. If we did that we could pick some hazelnuts on the way back.

I got on it first and walked across. It was a big, wide tree and Meggie waited till I was off, then she started across. She got half-way, when a foot skidded, the soles of the shoes were new and smooth and one shoe fell off into the water. She got across quickly and we both jumped into the burn, thinking we could remember where the shoe fell and go straight to the spot. When we got there, we could see no shoe. We went round and round in ever widening circles but still no shoe. We paddled down the burn with our skirts hiked up but we never found the shoe. Poor Meggie had to walk home with only one shoe. She was dreading telling her mother. She never did tell me how she got on.

I liked Meggie's mam, she was a widow, who bred dogs in her back garden. She had a big pen leading into a shed, in which the dogs were kept. The first time I was in Meggie's kitchen waiting for her to go out to play, she was stirring a huge pot of something that smelt so tasty. I asked her if she was cooking the tea for her mam. She laughed, saying no, she was preparing the dogs' feed. I thought that she was kidding me, it smelled too good for the dogs. She said that it was something called 'lites', which her mam got from the butcher. So it was animal intestines not for human consumption. But, I said, "It smells so good, what else is in it?" She said that I was smelling Oxo cubes. I had to have a look at these as I had never heard of them. She showed me the cube and crumbled it into a cup of boiling water, stirred it like a cup of tea and I had a taste. I'd never tasted anything like it before. I told mam about this great cube for cooking but she still kept to the old Bisto.

One of the first items on my first shopping list when I got married years later was Oxo cubes.

WE were into our autumn mode of games now. We had different games for each season. Autumn meant dark nights, so we used to gather under the lamp in the squarie and decide what we were going to play. Most of the time it would be a game called 'leev-oh'. The den would be the lamp post in the squarie, which you had to touch. One person would be in the den and everyone else would hide. A grown up version of hide and seek. We always put boundaries on it, like no crossing the ford, Scottie's field, Roysvale field and Hanton's shop. One person who got to the squarie light could let anyone who had been caught in the den be free again. This game could go on for nights on end, starting where we left off. Eventually we were venturing so far away from the den that we had to put High Street out of bounds. It was great fun in the dark and some of the boys who were in the choir with us and in the same class in school used to come down and join in the fun.

There was as usual, choir practice and silly games with Smithie. We went to the pictures more in the dark nights and we all used to gather down the front in the ninepenny seats. These were the cheapest seats in the picture house and they were solid wood. The boys would always sit in the row behind us girls and if you had a crush on anyone you always hoped he would sit behind you. We were all at that embarrassing age. I remember having this crush on a boy from Findhorn, who was called *'tattie bogle'* and I was sure he had a crush on me. I would only ever see him at the pictures but he always made sure he got the seat behind me. This went on all one winter. He was a year ahead of me in school and always smiled at me in the playground but most of the Findhorn boys always stuck together, so I just saw him at the pictures.

I was very saddened to hear that he was killed on his motorbike on the way to work in Inverness when he was 16.

I MUST say more about my extended family here. Uncle Wilson was married to Isabel McCandie, Auntie Maggie was married to a farmer called Don and I spent a week with them in Aberdeen. Auntie Maggie took me ice skating at the ice rink for the first time. Auntie Margaret, Hugh's wife and Uncle Hugh had another daughter called Sandra and Uncle Charlie and Auntie Helen had a son called Michael. Uncle Davy was to be married shortly.

Auntie Margaret and Jimmy had a baby, wee Jimmy and they got a flat in a big house called Clairmont, which sat in its own grounds on North Road. I often visited them, I still felt close to Auntie Margaret. They lived there for a little while until they got a prefab at Fleurs Place. They were to live there for a few years and I used to babysit for them as I got older.

One of my strongest memories of them when they were still living with us was Jimmy buying a car. It was to carry his dance band around to all the dances. It was a huge old thing and he kept it where the beginning of Roysvale Terrace and Castle Street join up. In the winter nights when it was too cold, even for us, to play out for long, Meggie and I used to go and sit in the back seat and gossip. It was quite luxurious, all leather inside and so comfy. It was never locked in those days. No one needed to lock any doors, there was never such a thing as stealing from your neighbours, let alone anyone else. Uncle Jimmy was now entertaining the pensioners every Wednesday down Cumming Street, in the YMCA.

I would go there every Wednesday after school and sing for them. I'd get a cup of tea and a biscuit. They were always pleased to see us.

Forres was still very much a small town. MacDonald Drive had been built and Ferry Road was on the cards to be built. Mannachie Terrace would be the last, people were still living in the huts up there.

With the RAF married quarters being built at Kinloss, there were a lot of new faces in our school and we had a good mixture of Scottish and English kids now. That made for quite a bit of rivalry between the boys. They all stayed in their own groups but us girls mixed more with the incomers. I also think that it made us more competitive in the classroom. To keep your place in class you had to work harder.

I enjoyed most of our curriculum but what I didn't like was science. We had a young male teacher, who we used to call 'pinhead' because he had a weird looking head and a very thin body. He used to walk around us with a Bunsen burner tube in his hand and if he thought you were not paying attention, he would smack you over the knuckles with it. I was dreading getting a smack because I nearly always fell asleep in his class. The classroom was so warm, especially in summer when the sun shone directly in the windows.

One of my favourite subjects was geography. We were often allowed National Geographic magazines to look at and it was great to learn about the rest of the world. With no TV yet, it was the only way to learn about the world and its people. We also had to draw maps of countries, what produce these countries grew and exported to us from the area where they were grown. We also had to make a scrapbook and put all the labels we could find of tins of food that had been imported to our country, such as corned beef from Argentina. There was great rivalry among us because the best scrapbook would get a small prize.

I seemed to have an aptitude for map drawing and was asked to draw a map of Forres High Street in detail, including every street and close. I had a great time doing it and it was hung in the archives in the Tolbooth for a few years. It's not there now and I do not know what happened to it.

Autumn was with us again and we girls would be picking brambles, climbing trees for hazelnuts and the boys would be out looking for chestnuts. We were always to be found somewhere up the burn or Sanquhar exploring. We would often meet Mrs Edwards and if she was in her car driven by her chauffeur she would stop and speak to us. She never minded that we played on her land, she always said make sure we didn't do any damage and we never went too close to the house.

One time she opened her house to the public. Us girls went as we were dying to see the gardens because they looked so enticing from the outside. It was sixpence to get in, we had coffee and cake in the conservatory attached to the side of the house and we felt very grown up.

The gardens were beautiful, with a specie of tree that hung down to

Linda, Brenda & Violet 1955

the ground, which you could walk under the canopy of and no-one could see you. Wild flowers were everywhere, ones we never knew the names of. It was just a paradise for kids to play in.

When the old lady passed away, the house was rented out in flats but eventually it had to be pulled down because of dry rot. It was never the same again, although the grounds were still quite beautiful. I was so sad to hear years later that the grounds were sold to build houses on, probably to strangers who will never know what it looked like in its heyday.

October came round again, time for tattie holidays and I got three weeks exemption from school to pick tatties on local farms. Even though I did not enjoy it the year before, I decided that I needed the money. It was a long three weeks and hard work, even though we were all fit. I was glad when the three weeks were up and I could go back to school. Mam let me buy my first pair of jeans with my tattie money and I was so proud of them I strutted about like a peacock in front of mam's mirror. I could only find out about fashion trends by reading mam's magazines and looking at catalogues. We were really cut off from the rest of the country in that respect. As for pop idols like today, we didn't hear much about them, the wireless in those days was all about Workers' Playtime. (**Workers' Playtime** *was a radio variety programme transmitted by the BBC between 1941 and 1964. Originally intended as a morale-booster for industrial workers in Britain during World War II, the programme was broadcast at lunchtime, three times a week, live from a factory canteen "somewhere in Britain". In all its 23 years each show concluded with the words from the show's producer, Bill Gates: "Good luck, all workers!" The programme had the support of the government because the shows were seen as supporting the war effort. Many famous variety, vocal and comedy artists appeared over the years.*)

LONG ago we led quite insular lives in Moray in the north-east of Scotland, having everything we needed in our own little towns. We never needed to go outwith the towns for anything except to go to hospital, which in those days was in Inverness. We may have seemed a bit backward to outsiders, or just plain old-fashioned but we were quite cut off from the rest of the country and the other little towns around us were probably the same. It was just our way of life. Things started to change slowly with the advent of young RAF servicemen to Kinloss and Lossiemouth. They brought with them the fashion in men's clothing, the new look, the first real changes since the war years. We were very curious about these changes, the draped jacket, the drainpipe trousers and the DA *(duck's arse!)* haircuts. The height of sophistication, as we saw it.

In the spring of 1956 I was 14 years old and looking ahead, I had just one more year of school. My friend Jeannie would be leaving in the summer, Gladys would be gone and that left me, Mavis and Violet of the old gang still at school. My friend Meggie had left and was working in an orphanage in Rothes. Quite suddenly we were on the verge of adulthood. We stopped playing games, started taking long walks on a

Sunday, usually up to Grant Park and round Cluny Hill. Of course we met up with boys we knew from school. They would be out for a stroll as well and there was always a lot of giggling - we were like all teenagers the world over. We usually gravitated to the swings in the park. Then we would go into the Forres House rest rooms, to sit and giggle some more; if anyone had a cigarette we would all have a puff and feel very grown up, probably very sick if truth be known.

I think Jeannie was the first of us to have a camera, a box Brownie, so we had fun taking pictures and posing. That spring mam had bought me a duffle coat, which was all the rage that year, so I had to have my photo taken in it. I wore that coat till it was threadbare, I was so proud of it.

As I said earlier, it was difficult for us girls to find out what the fashion was in the big cities. Mam used to get the *Red Star* and *Secrets* magazines for young women and I used to scour the pages for any tips. In those days us girls were never allowed to wear make-up of any kind until we left school, so it was a bit of a mystery to us as to how you put it on. When mam wasn't about I used to have a wee shot of her stuff but all I got was a clown looking back at me from the mirror. Also, at this age we were not allowed to wear stockings, or nylons, as they were called. A year later, once we were of age to wear stockings, we had to wear a 'roll-on', which had suspenders attached. This was worn before more comfortable suspender belts had been invented. It looked like a pantie-girdle but it had no crotch. It was made of heavy elastic and we had to roll it on. This was difficult – we had to put it on over our thighs and then roll it over our stomach up to the waist. It was so uncomfortable. The stockings would be attached to the suspenders.

Of course, as I said earlier, we saw the fashions for men because of the RAF camp just down the road. Our town was flooded with young airmen who dressed as Teddy Boys. We were quite in awe of them. This was the latest fashion for men and they looked so strange to me. They wore drainpipe trousers, which were tight all the way down from hip to ankle, thick-soled crepe shoes, a draped jacket, usually worn down to mid-thigh with velvet lapels, a shirt and string tie. Their hair would be thick and slicked back with Brilliantine in the style of James Dean, the heartthrob of the big screen. These boys never smiled because James Dean never smiled and it was a kind of scary feeling if you passed one in the street. Mam was once again warning me to stay away from these boys as they were just hooligans in her opinion. Parents were outraged at the new fashion for men. She needn't have worried though because I found them quite funny in their getup.

We would all go to the pictures once a week and hope to see some of the new pop singers in America. We were excited about the new wave of film stars we were beginning to see on the screen. The English stars were a bit boring to us but if there was an American film on you would see us all down in the front seats.

THIS year saw a major change to our High Street. The café culture arrived in Forres with the opening of the Lido Café. To us girls it was a big event, we spoke about it endlessly. I was told by mam to cross the street when I came up to it and not even look at it. That made it all the more intriguing to me and I wondered why it should be out of bounds. Wonder of wonders, it had a jukebox, which none of us had ever seen, let alone know how it worked but we could hear pop music coming out of the café all day long. We were bursting with curiosity to see inside but I was scared to go in because mam thought it was a den of iniquity. Of course it was always full of RAF boys, so it was definitely a no-go for me. But my Uncle Jimmy took me in there one time and I thought I was the bees knees, sitting there drinking coffee. I had never tasted coffee before and it was like Manna to me. I didn't tell mam where I'd been, she would have had a fit.

There was one time I was off school because mam was ill, friends were coming to visit her and she sent me up the town for a packet of biscuits. I thought this is my chance to go into the Lido again because they sold biscuits. As I was standing at the counter, I could hear giggling coming from round the corner in the café, up at the back. I knew there were booths up there because Uncle Jimmy had got us a seat up the side. I was sure I recognised a voice and I could see part of a face and hair I recognized. I walked up to the back and there was my friend Ellen, with a few of her mates in the back booth. They'd been jooking the school *(playing truant)*. I thought they were very brave to do this and to be in the Lido, because we had been warned by the headmaster not to go there in school time. I had barely arrived at the booth when I heard footsteps coming up behind me. It was Mrs Sharp, Ellen's mother. Someone had told her that Ellen was in the Lido. My heart was in my mouth, I didn't know what to do. Mrs Sharp grabbed Ellen by the ear and marched her out of the café. As they were leaving, Mrs Sharp looked at every one of us and said she knew all our mothers and she would be telling them about us being there and she would also tell the headmaster. I had to explain my way out of this pickle to him and mam and, in this instance, I was believed. It was quite scary though.

With the summer holidays came an offer of another job. The lady who owned the chip shop beside Ashers the bakers, which is now a Chinese takeaway, had asked mam if I would like a wee job in the evenings. I went to see her and she told me the hours would be from 4pm through to 9pm. I thought I could manage that and I liked the woman, so I started straight away. I was to work through the back of the shop, using a machine to peel the potatoes and then cut the eyes out - what a boring job. It took forever to do them and it was an ongoing job. I had my tea there and I could have anything I wanted. Sometimes I would work in the main shop selling the chips. I liked it there once I got over my shyness of having to face people head on. All was going great and I was gaining confidence with the public, when the lady boss said she would have to let me go, because I was under age to work these particular hours. I was a bit disappointed but I was also free to see my friends in the evenings again - I had missed that.

This summer would be the last of our childhood and it was a special time for us all because none of us knew what we would be doing in a years' time, although we all knew that we would be leaving school and hopefully working for a living. Jeannie and Meggie had already left the group and were working, Meggie at the orphanage up at Rothes and Jeannie had a live-in job at the Carlton Hotel.

The gap between childhood and adulthood was closing very quickly now and by the time we were 15, we would be treated as young adults with responsible jobs. We all matured more quickly than our counterparts today, we had no other choice.

That last summer of our childhood, we still had a lot of fun. Although we didn't play games anymore, we still had the freedom to roam about Forres. We were often up Cluny Hill on long walks, or up the burn, which we never tired of. On rainy days we would hole up in someone's shed, discuss make up and fashion, talk about our latest boy craze and always music. There was a little shop where a charity shop is today, that used to sell books and song magazines with the words to popular songs. I was always in there getting the latest one. We would learn the words to them and sing them together. We were so frustrated that we couldn't get enough information about the pop idols of that era. TV hadn't come to Forres in a big way yet. We'd only ever seen it in Younie's window around the time of the Coronation in 1953. No-one we knew had a telly. Everyone had a wireless, with those heavy dried batteries that I still collected for Mrs McDonald.

Our latest craze now was to learn to rock and roll. We knew that it was out there somewhere but couldn't get much information about how to do it. Violet's sister Gladys would try and show us how to do it but we couldn't get the hang of it. We just didn't have the right music to dance to. We never saw anyone dance it and we were never allowed to go to the dances, so we were only hearing about it. The young airmen up from the south were teaching the girls how to do it. We knew the songs that were popular for dancing to because we often sneaked to the Lido for a quick drink. The music was such a draw because pop songs were never played on the radio and we never saw pop singers at the cinema. We only saw Doris Day or Bobby Darin in films.

At this age, clothes became important to us girls. Catalogues were where we got a lot of ideas of what was in fashion. We would pore over any we could get our hands on. As I said before duffle coats were the fashion for the winter when we were 14. I was desperate to have one, so mam said if I worked at the tatties, I could pay for half and she would pay the rest. I was over the moon, even though it meant back-breaking work again. The day I got it I couldn't wait to show the rest of the girls. I wore that coat till it was threadbare.

Another fashion of the day was a flared felt skirt, sometimes with an appliquéd patch on it. We saw Sandra Dee, an American actress, wearing them in films and they were a must too. She later married pop idol, Bobby Darin.

Along with these new fashions, we still had to wear socks because we were still considered children. We were never allowed to wear makeup of any sort and never, ever, lipstick! Of course, mam used makeup, so I did get to practice with her old stuff but could never show my face out the door with it on.

Of course, we were all jealous of Meggie, Jeannie and Gladys, who were now young women who could wear all these things because they had left school and were working. Us girls were just chomping at the bit to start being young women.

Avertisement for Oxo 1951

Chapter 17
1956-1957

The last autumn term of my final school year began quietly. I couldn't wait to finish. At the end, it didn't matter what exams I would be sitting because there would be no certificates to show what standard of education I'd reached. Because I had to leave school at 15, I couldn't sit 'O' Levels, which were taken when you were 16. I had to leave school to earn money. I still enjoyed learning though and that helped to get me through the last year.

That year I went on the tatties for the last time to earn money. It was worth the back-breaking work but I swore I would never do that again. My brother Jimmy and I did the usual picking of rasps for the sewing teacher and we shared the money we earned. My money went on winter boots this year. I was growing up and realised that if I wanted new clothes or footwear that weren't hand-me-downs I would have to help pay for them myself. With so many kids in our house, money was always at a premium.

Of course, I still had my wee jobs going - Mrs McDonald's shopping and the Sunday paper round. Believe it or not, through all the hard times, mam and dad still gave us a few pennies pocket money. Jimmy and I had to earn ours, being the oldest. But things got better for the other kids when first I, then later Jimmy, left school and brought money into the home.

That winter was a cold one, it was always below zero. We all had chapped hands and chilblains. I had chilblains up the front of my legs and it was just agony in bed at night, I just wanted to scratch when my legs got warmed up. I can tell you this took a long time, with only one fire going in the house. We got used to having practically no heating in the house but it was difficult with such low temperatures. The stone houses seemed to absorb the cold from the outside and every morning we rose to ice flower patterns on all the windows. We learned to get dressed very quickly!

The milk was always frozen on the door step and the robins had been at the silver tops. Somehow they knew what was in these bottles. Thinking back, it seems amazing that the milk cart always made it through the snow, no matter how bad a night it had been. Nowadays, people simply wouldn't turn out in those conditions. The schools very seldom closed whatever the weather, unless there were blizzards. If the outlying kids were snowed in that was just their luck. I often wished we'd get snowed in at Roysvale!

All kids suffered from the cold in those days. Boys had to wear short trousers up until they went to the Academy, or even longer, depending on their parents views but us girls never got to wear trousers at all. No such thing as tights, it was bare legs all the way. At least next winter I'd be able to wear nylons! I consoled myself through that last winter with this comforting thought.

Christmas was now in the offing and I had a lot of parties to look forward to. Our choir entertained the old folks and we sang at the hospital too. We all loved that time of year, singing the old Christmas carols. We had the Christmas party to come, as well as the army, air force and scout parties. All us girls were always invited by whichever boys had a crush on you at that time. The highlight of the year was the school dance, particularly for us as third formers who were nearly grown up. Through the winter months in our PE lessons we were taught modern dancing. In previous years we were taught Scottish dancing, modern waltzes, quicksteps, foxtrots and definitely not rock and roll!

Mam had really pushed the boat out and bought me a party dress out of a catalogue. I couldn't wait to wear it. It was made of baby pink taffeta, hanging just below my shins, with frills round the hem, neck and sleeves. It was a beautiful dress but I just wasn't a baby pink and frills girl - when I put it on I knew I'd grown - it was too tight round the bust. But mam was over the moon and she loved how I looked in it. I knew I couldn't say anything to disappoint her, as it wouldn't have been cheap. I got myself all ready to go to the dance, showed dad and the family how I looked and off I set to meet my friends and off we went. I knew from the first dance that I was going to have trouble breathing in this frock, I could almost hear the seams creaking as I danced, striving to keep my breathing shallow, saying to myself 'no deep breaths'. I couldn't believe this was happening to me, my first new dress since the Coronation and mam didn't think to measure me. By the end of the night I was just about expiring from little breaths and lack of air! But I grimly wore that dress to all the parties, for mam's sake.

WHEN Hogmanay *(Scottish celebration of New Year's Eve)* came round, I was finally old enough to stay up till after midnight and babysit the kids to let mam and dad go up to the Cross for the first time in years. It was always a great thing to look forward to in those years. Old friends would meet and greet. It was a time for the grown ups to let their hair down and enjoy a dram, vodka was unheard of in those years and everybody had their half bottle of whisky. Some members of the pipe band would be playing, some folks singing *'Auld Lang Syne'*, some folks dancing but everyone having a good old time. At the end of it all, there was always a shop window cracked or broken. Uncle Wilson got the blame for it one year, which he denies doing to this day.

After all the high jinx, everyone went first footing to neighbours and friends, where the partying continued on for the next 24 hours. *('First footing' or the 'first foot' in the house after midnight is common across Scotland. To ensure good luck for the house the first foot should be a dark male and he should bring with him symbolic pieces of coal, shortbread, salt, black bun and a wee dram of whisky.)* In Scotland in those days people only got 1st January as a holiday and there were a lot of 'sair heiddies' *(sore heads)* going back to work. Usually some of mam's family came by and I was allowed to stay up to see them. It was a merry time and great fun for me, being allowed up so late. But all good times have to end and we were into January and still facing a cold bitter winter.

This New Year Uncle Wilson was home on leave from the army and he liked his dram. He was up at the Cross like everyone else, celebrating and he says he saw the broken window of DE shoe shop and having had more than a few, he decided to try some shoes on and stepped through the broken window. He was sitting down trying a pair on when Sergeant Dan Tulloch, the town bobby found him. He denied vehemently that it was him that broke the window but he was taken to the police cells for the night. He was very upset about this as he had only a couple of weeks till demob *(finishing National Service)* and this if the case went to court, it would affect his reference from the Army. Finally Dan Tulloch relented and let him go with many warnings about good behaviour in future.

The next six months were a long slow drag for me, like time had been suspended. This year was to be the most important year so far in my life and I wasn't sure how to deal with it.

Smithie the Minister had asked me if I would like to join the senior choir and I said I would. I started going to choir practices in the Sunday school hall but it wasn't the same. I missed all the old choir members and all the laughs we had. I was the youngest among all these grown-ups and there was no fun in them, they were too solemn. It felt strange to be sitting with them on Sundays in church, looking down on my old choir.

As we headed towards the Easter holidays and the lighter nights, I always had to revise for one exam or another. It always felt great to be able to shed some layers of clothing as the days got milder although it was not unusual to wake up to snow on a May morning.

After the two weeks holiday for Easter, it was back to school for the last lap as far as I was concerned. Two more months of school and I would be a free woman. I knew mam and dad wouldn't let me stay on, so I would have to think about what to do with my life. There was not a lot to think about as there were few choices in our wee town. All us girls were of the same opinion. We were almost like horses at the starting gate, pawing the ground. We would go to bed one night as children and get up the next day as young adults, the gates would be open and the race would be on for jobs. But until then, we had two more months of school and exams at the end. I was determined to do well in my last exams, if only for my own satisfaction.

In those last two months, we seemed to grow up quickly. We would be out and about all weekend, in Grant Park, up the 'hill', having sly puffs of fags in Forres House and always flirting with the boys, who would be doing the same things. We were always having mad crushes on some boy or other and arrange to meet them in the picture house the next weekend in the ninepenny seats. That night there was always a rush to get the best seats and, as I said before, you never sat with the boy you had the crush on, he had always to sit directly behind you. You would never, ever be seen holding hands. That was a complete no no. You would be the talk of the town in no time!

US girls were still sneaking coffees in the Lido café at the weekends and listening to the latest pop songs, learning the words of the songs and we would sing them when we were out for walks. It was round about this time that I met a young man called Dave. He was 18 years old and had just come up to Kinloss out of the Boy Entrants in the RAF. The Boy Entrants joined up when they were 16-18 years of age and then they passed out as fully fledged airmen. They were then posted all over the UK and Dave was posted to Kinloss.

There were quite a few boys of that age, who were posted to Kinloss and quite a few knew each other and so us girls got to know them quite well.

Dave became my steady boyfriend, although my parents never knew about him for quite a while. But once I finished school I told them about him, how old he was and where he came from. After a while he started calling for me at my house and mam and dad got to know him and liked him. He was even good with the kids, he having a little sister under school age himself. But I still liked to be with my friends and so some of his friends of the same age and my friends would often get together for coffee in the Lido and we would gossip and have fun, drinking endless coffees. I did know that this was an interim period, a few weeks grace. I knew I had to start looking for employment. Mam had been good to me, letting me have this time out, to get used to being a young woman but playtime was over.

Chapter 18
1957

I had intended to finish this story when I left school at 15, forgetting the fact that my family history didn't end there. There was a member of the family still to be born. So I will continue for one more year.

My circle of friends had grown over the years spent at the Academy, with the influx of children from the country schools around us and Kinloss and Findhorn villages. One of the girls was Rosemary who was going out with a friend of Dave's. She worked at Gordonstoun School, which was in Altyre then, just outside Forres. She said there was a job going and would I be interested. It meant I had to buy a bike because it was off the beaten track and no buses went up there. I got the job but I didn't like it at all, it involved housework and cooking and one day off a week. If I wanted to go out at night I'd have to cycle in the dark. That was scary, especially if I was cycling back late at night through the woods. Sometimes we would all cycle together but often I would be alone and my imagination used to work overtime.

I had to hang onto this job or have another one lined up, because I had bought my bike on the never never *(hire purchase)* from Stuart's the cycle agent. It was a brand new Raleigh, bright red and I was chuffed to bits with it.

I used to moan to mam about the job, I really hated it but I knew I couldn't hand in my notice or I would lose my bike and I would still have to earn a living. I was at home one day in the autumn and mam came home with great news. Mattie Sandison, who owned the West End paper shop where mam got all her papers and magazines, asked mam if I would like a job in her shop. I went for an interview and got the job. I worked one week's notice at Gordonstoun and started the following Monday. *(Gordonstoun School eventually expanded and relocated to Duffus where it is today. Prince Philip, the Duke of Edinburgh, Princes Charles, Andrew and Edward attended this school as well as Princess Anne's children, Zara and Peter. It has been documented that Prince Charles hated his time there.)*

Well, I just hated this job too! I started at 7am in the morning, got from 9am till 10am off for breakfast, worked from 10am till 1pm, got one hour off for lunch, then worked from 2pm till 6pm, with a half day Wednesday. I was working a 50 hour week for one pound, seventeen shillings and sixpence *(£1.87)* per week.

Mam got one pound and I had the rest. I was stuck through the back of the shop writing names on hundreds of papers and magazines. Miss Sandison was a right tartar to work for, it seemed I could do nothing right. I had to wear an overall with long sleeves which she didn't provide, so I got one of my Aunt Maggie's, as she had some for working at the Plasmon Mill. It was dark green with a belt, down to mid leg. I thought it might keep me a bit warmer in the back of the shop but my hands were still blue with cold. That winter I had chilblains on my fingers as well as on my feet and legs. In those days we were never allowed to wear trousers to work, it was unheard of and stockings and suspenders never kept you warm.

Finally, Miss Sandison thought it was time for me to work in the front of the shop. When my work was done through the back, I would serve at the counter, with her teaching me the till. I really liked it then, meeting all the people who came in. She had a big lot of regulars who came in every day. In the early morning the men going to work would come in and buy cigarettes and newspapers. Housewives would come in during the day. The shop stocked and sold paperback books and I was in my element sorting them all out and stacking the shelves.

Miss Sandison never trusted anyone where money was concerned and it was such a bind having to show her the change for every customer. As I was learning how to go about my job, I did notice that she didn't treat every customer the same and I began to watch her in action. I must tell you here that she was a spinster, late fifties I think, about five foot nothing, quite squat, with mousey brown hair rolled up at the ends like during the war. She was also very short-sighted and wore glasses that looked like bottle ends. She always dressed in tweed suits and brogues. When an attractive man came into the shop she would rush to push me aside so that she could serve him.

Next door to our shop was a grocer called Philp and Mr Philp was a tall well-preserved man in his prime, swept back silver hair and, looking back, quite attractive, though old enough to be my father. When he came in each day for his papers, she would rush to serve him and she used to look up into his face and simper. That's the only word to describe it. I used to have to look away as I was bursting to laugh! If she saw him out on the pavement she would rush outside to talk to him.

KENNY Ball and his Jazzmen came quite often to Forres, The Clyde Valley Stompers were a firm favourite and we even had Screaming Lord Sutch, who came onto the stage with a toilet seat round his neck! The local bands were excellent too. Alex Sutherland and his band, Nat Fraser and his band were all brilliant musicians and great vocalists. A few years later, a new dancehall opened in Elgin, the next town twelve miles away, called The Two Red Shoes and it was a great success. A crowd of us used to go quite regularly and catch the last bus home. It vied with Forres to get the best groups. One night in particular we all went to hear this group called The Beatles and had a good laugh about the name. If someone was to tell us they were to become a worldwide success we would have laughed, for although they were good, so were all the rest of the bands coming our way.

As I said earlier, there was no shortage of jobs for us who left school at 15, the boys going into apprenticeships and the girls into various shops and hotels in town. All of us, except those who worked in hotels, had a half day off on Wednesdays and we mostly met up in the Lido to exchange our news and moan about our jobs. By this time we were going to the local dances and that was a favourite topic of conversation. We were very lucky because Forres had become a very popular place for the dances. Many of the big bands from all over the country used to come and perform in the town hall every Thursday, Friday and Saturday. Buses came from as far away as Inverness. We girls used to live for these nights. On Thursdays and Fridays the dances went on until 1am and 11.30pm on Saturdays. There was also a great dance every Monday night in the Fisherman's Institute in Buckie, about 25 miles down the coast, with a free bus from Kinloss. But we had to walk back to Forres from Kinloss - about four miles - usually in high heels, in the early hours and turned up for work knackered the next morning. We also used to go to dances in Burghead and the Tradespark in Nairn. We just loved the dances, because the bands were modern and rock and roll and jiving were all the rage. We used to wear felt skirts with layers of frilly net petticoats and ballerina shoes on our feet. We really relished the freedom we all had now.

During the last summer holidays before I started work, I realised that there was an atmosphere around the home. Mam and dad were always arguing, shouting at the kids, or not speaking for long periods. It dawned on me that mam was getting fatter and I asked her straight out was she expecting and she had to tell me she was. I suppose in a lot of ways it was a relief to tell someone. I knew that she didn't want another baby, she must have been sick to death with nappies. Everything was washed by hand in those days and I still remember her hands all red and shiny from constantly being in water.

I asked her outright why was she having another baby, wasn't she miserable enough with all she'd got (the callousness of youth) and she told me that dad didn't believe in birth control. Well, I was so angry with him I never spoke to him if I could avoid it. This went on for months.

I was not speaking to him and mam was not speaking to him, so he must have been going through his own hell and most probably getting a talking to from Granny Fraser, who he visited every Saturday or Sunday. They all knew that there was to be a new baby somewhere down the line because back in the late spring mam and dad, Auntie Margaret, Hugh's wife and Uncle Hugh had been for an afternoon Sunday visit and my cousin Violet had been invited too. They often had this gathering and cousin Violet would read everyone's tea leaves. She said then that there was to be a new baby and of course both mam and Auntie Margaret denied they were expecting. Mam didn't know at that time but cousin Violet was never wrong and of course it was mam again.

Jean, Jimmy, David & Raymond *(back row)*
Dad, Auntie Margaret & Jimmy *(middle row)*
Fiona, Alan, Wee Jimmy, Wendy & Wee Margaret *(front row)*

Chapter 19
1958

Mum & Dad with baby Alan

In the first week of 1958, my youngest brother Alan was born, at home as usual with the long-suffering friend Helen in attendance once again. I don't know what mam would have done without Helen. She was a very dear friend to mam and completely unflappable. I never ever saw her in a panic and better than any doctor or midwife. Dr Bethune always knew that she was there so he never came until it was all over. The only good thing about it all was mam must have had easy births because she never needed any attention either before or after the births.

So, here we were again, another bawling baby, the house bursting at the seams with bodies. I took myself away as often as I could, I couldn't stand the constant noise, the kids fighting, the baby crying and mam shouting at everyone. You could hear it all half way down the road. I could have found my way home blindfolded, just by following the noise.

That was a miserable, cold winter and I spent my spare time with my friends and boyfriend Dave. He was to be going on a course for nine months in the south of England and I knew that I would miss him so much. He left at the beginning of February and we wrote every day. He said that he wondered if mam and dad would let me come down and live with his parents so that he could see me every weekend. He said that he had asked his parents and they would be writing to mam.

The outcome of it all was that I was to go down to England. Dave came up to Forres and took me down to Kirkby-in-Ashfield, a few miles out of Nottingham. His parents were lovely people and made me feel like one of the family. Mrs Sharpe had even got me an interview for a job in the next town, just a couple of miles along the road. So at the beginning of the next week, she and I took the bus to Sutton-in-Ashfield, where I had my interview.

It was in one of the big old fashioned drapery stores and I'll tell you now, every time I watch *'Are you being served'* on the TV it brings me right back to where I worked all those years ago.

The job was for a cashier and was right up my street. I was chuffed to bits because I felt my education would have been wasted if I didn't get a good job, even though I had to leave before getting my 'O' levels. I was to be their book-keeper as well! All hail to Mrs Hay! I used to hate commercial subjects at school but she must have got it through to me. You must remember that I was not 16 until April so it was a major achievement for me. I was to be trained by this old woman who was retiring and then I was on my own, answerable only to the shop manager. He was a nice man, mid-thirties and I got on well with him.

To save on bus fares, Mrs Sharpe suggested that I get mam to send down my bike by train, as it was only a couple of miles to work, which mam duly did.

Every Friday night Dave would come home and leave on the Sunday night. I had to work Saturdays but on Sundays we would explore all over Derbyshire and Yorkshire with Dave's brother and fiancée, touring around in the parents' car.

MY place of work was called Dowells and it was a very classy shop. It was on one level and was very big. Although it was a drapery, it also was an accessory and corsetry shop. It had glass counters with drawers underneath with glass fronts that you could see into from in front of the counter. We sold scarves, gloves, evening bags and all manner of things wanted for weddings and formal occasions. The corsetry side was big business and one member of staff was trained at a special school in those days. That was Miss England, whose counter was right up beside my office and who was to become a very good friend. One of the rules of the shop was that we never called each other by our Christian names and I was always called Miss Fraser. Everyone became Miss this and Miss that, so much so, that when you met each other outside shop hours you automatically called them Miss etc. And just like in the comedy show, if someone needed help they would call politely, "Are you free Miss Fraser?" As well as cashier and the book-keeping duties, I was trained on all the counters so that I could help when there was a rush on and the manager would take over from me.

We all had to dress in black and white, normally black pencil slim skirt, white blouse, with a little black bow at the neck, a black cardigan if needed, black court shoes or stilettos and sheer nylons. We were all so very smart and solemn, we were not allowed to laugh or giggle. This was to be my world for the foreseeable future.

My office was something I'd never seen before. The shop was wide and long and at the back facing into the shop, perched about eight or nine feet above the floor, was my office, which had huge glass windows. It had steps leading up to a door into it. I sat at a big desk looking out over my little empire. I was the only one to handle cash. Every counter had a wire rail leading from there to me, well above the heads of everyone. Attached to the wires were metal cups which opened and closed with a twist. The counter assistants wrote out a carbon receipt for each item, put that and money into the metal cup and pulled a wooden handle hanging beside it. The cup whizzed along the rail to me in my box, I took out the contents and sent back the change, if any, by the same method. There were ten counters with wires all leading to me and, on a busy day, they would come thick and fast and it felt like I was milking cows endlessly! There was a constant noise of whizzing and clacking. It was fun to begin with but when I was trying to balance the books and continually being interrupted by the clanging above my head it wasn't so funny.

As I said earlier, I was trained to work at all the counters, so it was fun to get a break away from the book-keeping and serve the customers. I liked the book-keeping but I had to do it all with pen and ink, the old fashioned way and at the end of the day I was always covered in ink. We had a staff room up in the attic and I usually had my packed lunch there.

Although Dave came home every Friday, I was missing my family, kids and all! I was missing Forres and the countryside around. There were no hills to see here, very little countryside, it was all built up, with one town leading into the other. The girls from work made me very welcome, taking me out to the occasional dance or to the pictures, which made it less lonely. At Easter, they had a big parade where they dressed up in all their best clothes, made Easter bonnets and paraded about in their finery. I enjoyed all these new customs, so different from my Easters with the kids.

Mam was sending me the Forres Gazettes and the Forres news so I was keeping up with all the local goings on and she always wrote to me once a week, which I always looked forward to. But all it did was make me feel more homesick. My friend Jeannie wrote regularly, giving me all the gossip, who was seeing who, who had split up with their boyfriend, all the dances they were going to and when was I coming home? I was allowed one week off in June, so I was definitely going home.

The weeks went by so slowly but finally the end of June came. Dave was coming home with me for a short break too and I was so excited to see everyone. I think those last few miles down the railway track from Dunphail to Forres were always the most heartfelt part of all my journeys home and this was to be the first of many for me over my lifetime but the feeling never changed.

We intended to take a taxi from the station but mam was there with all the kids and Alan in his high pram. What a welcome! But it meant that we had to walk carrying our cases all the way to Roysvale and I felt I'd arms like a gorilla by the time we got home! Mam had laid on a lovely afternoon tea for us and I finally knew I was a grown up. The kids couldn't wait to get stuck in but weren't allowed to until Dave and I had first serving. Mam had obviously saved her hard-earned pennies for this feast and the kids were watering at the mouth for their turn. I didn't keep them waiting long, I was so excited to be home.
I have never felt so happy in my life to be in my own home, never mind the tight squeeze with all of our bodies. I was back in my old wee room sharing a bed with my sister Jean again.

My baby brother Alan had only been a few weeks old when I left and now he was six months old and a fat little bundle. He was always laughing and wanting attention and he grew on me that week. I noticed that the rest of the kids seemed to have shot up too. The one I saw the most grown up was my oldest brother Jimmy. He had just finished his first year in the Academy and was in long trousers and proud of it. Mam told me that Fiona was still having tantrums about not being the baby anymore and dad was still fussing over her when she threw one and the other kids were getting the blame for starting her off. It seems some things never change.

Dave and I met all our friends again, his from the camp and mine from the town. We all had great fun; coffees in the Lido and going to the dances that were on that week. I took the kids for walks up the burn and round Sanquhar pond. It was great to be back.

Auntie Margaret & husband Jimmy,
with James, Wendy & Wee Margaret

Uncle Wilson came to visit and we went round to the prefabs to see Auntie Margaret who, as well as James, now had two girls, Wendy and wee Margaret, as she was to be called all her life.

I also paid my Granny Fraser a visit with mam, who went there every week. She never changed, always looked like time had passed her by, same with Grandad Fraser. She still had the sweetie jar full of thruppennies and my cousin Sheila was now doing her shopping at the wee shop on the corner.

I had packed so much into that week and suddenly it was time to go back down the road. I didn't want to go. But I couldn't stay, I owed it to my employers, so away I went, holding back the tears, with all my family around me.

I have always found throughout my life, that when the homesickness gets too much to bear, I must go home, just the once and the going back to wherever, no matter how hard it is at the time, gets easier to bear. No matter where you have to live your life, through choice or circumstance, the need to go back to your roots once in a while is a healthy and natural feeling. And that road home is as exciting as visiting a new and foreign land. I have always found it so.

But the day I left Forres again was heartbreaking for me. Being away had made me value what I was leaving behind this time. I was at very low ebb when I went back to my work. It seemed an endless time to October when I would be going home for good because this was when Dave would finish his fitter's course. We were into July now and the summer stretched endlessly ahead. Dave knew how I was missing home but didn't know what to do about it, except keep my spirits up every weekend. In the end, I knew that I had to go home for good. So at the end of August I returned home after working my notice, with a glowing reference from the manager for my next job. I didn't know what the future held for me but I knew that I wanted to spend the next few years with my family in Forres.

AFTER I came home from England, I'd been seeing more of my friend Ellen Sharp, whose family had moved from Burdshaugh to a house in Orchard Road. She had a job either in the Ramnee or the Park hotel and she usually had the afternoons free and we would meet up at her house for a gossip. One day I was walking round to my Granny Fraser's on the road by Anderson's school. I was just coming up to the High Street when I could see this person on a high bike coming along the road by Grant Park. As she drew nearer I saw it was Ellen. She cycled passed me waving her hand and she just looked like Mary Poppins. The bike must have come out of the ark, with its great big wheels and curved frame and there was Ellen perched on top, with a long navy gabardine coat on and her frilly waitress cap, part of her uniform, still on her head.

Ellen was always such a cheery person and saw the funny side of everything and the image of her on that bike still makes me smile.

Now that I was home again, I had to start looking for a job but meanwhile I just enjoyed the summer in Forres and helping my mam about the house and with Alan. It was a lovely time of year and I would take him for walks in his big high pram, or play with him in the back garden. All the kids were at school now so it was just the three of us. Once a week we would walk round to St Ronans Road to visit Granny Fraser. On one of those visits she told us that Auntie Connie was coming home from Canada in September with her four little sons, our cousins. Everyone was very excited, as none of my family had met Auntie Connie except me. I had been writing to her for a few years now and I was really looking forward to meeting her again after so many years. I was just a toddler when she left.

Meanwhile, I was still looking for a job but I didn't want to work in a shop or a hotel. I felt I'd had a good grounding in book-keeping and when a job in the East End post office was advertised in the Forres Gazette, I applied and got an interview. It was run then by Kenny McLennan, who was the sub postmaster. He told me that if I got the job I would be trained by his wife Margaret in all aspects of post office work. I gave him the reference from my old job and two days later he told me that I had got the job. I was delighted and the pay was more than I would have earned in a shop. As I trained and gained experience my pay was to increase and I eventually took over the running of it from Margaret.

I often went to see my friend Ellen in the evenings as she was still not old enough to train as a nurse. We often went to the Lido for coffee and to see other friends that we had grown up with, we were all still quite close. She was now working in The Forres Tearooms, where R & R Urquhart's is now. She didn't get half day Wednesday like me, so I used to go up to the tearooms about 2pm and she would sit me down at a table at the back, which was all set for afternoon tea. The place was always empty at this time. The table was set with a white tablecloth and napkins and out would come the cake stand with cakes, plates with sandwiches cut in triangles with crusts off and silver teapot and water jug. She would then take off her white frilly apron and cap and join me at the table. We would have our afternoon tea like ladies, with a lot of laughing and giggling. We did this every Wednesday while I worked in the town and no one ever found out about it.

Ellen was very much a fun person and would do anything for a laugh. I did miss her when she eventually went away to Glasgow to do her training. Years later she ended up nursing in Germany, at the same time I ended up at a RAF camp on the other side of Germany and we kept in touch.

Round about the time I started my new job, Dave had popped up for a weekend and we had a heart to heart talk. We decided we would stay good friends. He was a lovely boy and he continued to visit us all when he came back to Kinloss. My family was very fond of him and the kids really liked him, he was so good with them. Mam was very disappointed but I told her it was my life and choices had to be made by me alone. All us young men and women still met up in the Lido and we went to the local dances together and had a good time like teenagers do the world over. In the summer we all met up at Findhorn for a swim and picnics on the beach. In winter we used to have big snow fights up Grant Park. We still had a lot of child in us. I only wish that teenagers of today could enjoy the simple pleasures of being young, it only comes around once in a lifetime, then it's gone forever and you are left with the memories.

WELL that's more or less the story of my childhood. I trained for a year in the East End post office then went on to run the Kinloss post office. I studied for two years by enrolling on a correspondence course for the Civil Service and sat the examination in Inverness when I was eighteen. I was now a Postal and Telegraph Officer and could apply to banks for jobs now if I wanted a change. I had intended to but got married instead to Mike Stavert and we had two daughters, Lindsay and Joanne. We were married for 19 years.

Mike was in the RAF and was posted to Germany for two and a half years and then we came back to live in Edinburgh for about eight years. Whilst living in Edinburgh, I was shocked and very sad when mam wrote and told me that Jeannie had died. She was only in her early 30s and left a young family.

Over the years, I would come home to Forres for holidays, by plane, road and rail and that last two miles never ceased to thrill me. I would walk along the High Street and sure enough, I'd meet Ellen, or Jeannie, home like me for the holidays and visit Violet, who settled in Findhorn with her husband. Mavis worked away from home for a long time and I never did meet her again until she married Tex.

In 1971 we moved back to Forres when Mike was posted to RAF Kinloss and I have been here ever since.

In 1981 Mike and I parted, which was an unhappy period in my life. We divorced in 1985 and I married Gordon Green in 1986 and we are still together now. He was the one who encouraged me to write this book and he's been my rock through all the years. This book has been in my head since I was in my twenties and I felt compelled to write it. I've often wondered what other kids felt about living in these huts. There seems to be no record of this period of time in Forres so the story needed to be told.

MY school friends and my close friends have been scattered around the world at different times of their lives but most come home on holiday still, some come back to live here and others retire here. In the end, that says a lot for our little town, up here in Moray in the north-east of Scotland.

Auntie Connie, Uncle Hugh & Dad 1966

Violet with her mother, brothers sisters 1990
Left to right, Raymond, Jimmy, Violet, Fiona, Mother, Jean, David, Alan

About the Author

Violet Fraser was born during 1942 in a Forres hospital in the north-east of Scotland. In early childhood she and her mother, Jean, lived with grandparents, aunts and uncles in rural Moray until 1946 when her father returned from the war at the end of hostilities.

With nowhere to live the young family set up home in the huts in the old Burdshaugh prisoner of war camp. The families and wartime refugees that occupied these redundant huts were known locally - with equal degrees of affection and disdain - as 'squatters'. For Violet it was a formative period of a happy childhood.

Violet attended local schools whilst living at the huts, leaving education, age 15, to gain employment elsewhere in the UK before returning home to work in the local post office.

She married a RAF serviceman and had two daughters, subsequently living in Germany and Edinburgh before settling back in her home town.

Violet lives with her second husband, Gordon Green, within a stone's throw from her childhood home. Now retired, she felt compelled to tell the story of the squatters, these young men and women who survived the war and tried to make a home for their families in the most basic of conditions.